Preaching Through the Bible

Ephesians

Michael Eaton

Sovereign World

Sovereign World Ltd
PO Box 777
Tonbridge
Kent TN11 0ZS
England

ISBN 1 85240 310 1

Typeset by CRB Associates, Reepham, Norfolk.
Printed in England by Clays Ltd, St Ives plc.

By the same author:

Genesis 1–11 (Preaching Through the Bible) – Sovereign World

Genesis 12–23 (Preaching Through the Bible) – Sovereign World

Genesis 24–50 (Preaching Through the Bible) – Sovereign World

Applying God's Law (Exodus 19–24) – Paternoster

Joshua (Preaching Through the Bible) – Sovereign World

1 Samuel (Preaching Through the Bible) – Sovereign World

2 Samuel (Preaching Through the Bible) – Sovereign World

1 Kings (Preaching Through the Bible) – Sovereign World

Ecclesiastes (Tyndale Commentary) – IVP

Hosea (Focus on the Bible) – Christian Focus

Joel and Amos (Preaching Through the Bible) – Sovereign World

The Way That Leads to Life (Matthew 5 7) Christian Focus

Mark (Preaching Through the Bible) – Sovereign World

Luke 1–11 (Preaching Through the Bible) – Sovereign World

Return to Glory (Romans 3:22–5:21) – Paternoster

Living Under Grace (Romans 6–7) – Paternoster

1 Corinthians 1–9 (Preaching Through the Bible) – Sovereign World

1, 2 Thessalonians (Preaching Through the Bible) – Sovereign World

2 Timothy (Preaching Through the Bible) – Sovereign World

1 Peter (Preaching Through the Bible) – Sovereign World

1, 2, 3 John (Focus on the Bible) – Christian Focus

Living A Godly Life (Theology for Beginners) – Paternoster

Enjoying God's Worldwide Church (Theology for Beginners) – Paternoster

No Condemnation – IVCP (USA)

Experiencing God (Theology for Beginners) – Paternoster

Preface

There is need of a series of biblical expositions which are especially appropriate for English-speaking people throughout the world. Such expositions need to be laid out in such a way that they will be useful to those who like to have their material, or (if they are preachers), to put across their material, in clear points. They need to avoid difficult vocabulary and advanced grammatical structures. They need to avoid European or North American illustrations. *Preaching Through the Bible* seeks to meet such a need. Although intended for an international audience I have no doubt that their simplicity will be of interest to many first-language speakers of English as well. These expositions are based upon the Hebrew and Greek texts. The New American Standard Version and the New International Version of the Bible are recommended for the reader but at times the expositor will simply translate the Hebrew or Greek himself. In this book I provide my own translation of Ephesians.

It is not our purpose to deal with minute exegetical detail, although the commentator has to do work of this nature as part of his preliminary preparation. But just as a housewife likes to serve a good meal rather than display her pots and pans, so we are concerned with the 'good meal' of Scripture, rather than the 'pots and pans' of dictionaries, disputed interpretations and the like. Only occasionally will such matters have to be discussed. Similarly matters of introduction receive only as much attention as is necessary for the exposition to be clear. I ought to emphasise that simplicity of style is not simplicity of content. Although simply written on the surface these expositions aim at a high level of scholarship and attempt to put the theological and practical message of each book of the Bible in a clear and practical manner. God's word needs to be expounded with thoroughness but the language needs to remain easy and accessible. Some progress in this direction is attempted in these expositions. On occasions a simple outline of some introductory matters will be included, perhaps in an appendix, but the first chapter of each exposition gets into the message of Scripture as speedily as possible.

Contents

	Preface	5
	Author's Preface	9
Chapter 1	The Greatness of Salvation (Ephesians 1:1–14)	11
Chapter 2	Chosen To Be Holy (Ephesians 1:4–6a)	15
Chapter 3	A Mighty Plan (Ephesians 1:6b–10)	18
Chapter 4	Inheritance (Ephesians 1:11–14)	22
Chapter 5	Opened Eyes (Ephesians 1:15–19a)	26
Chapter 6	The Power of the Resurrection (Ephesians 1:19b–23)	29
Chapter 7	Dead – But Made Alive (Ephesians 2:1–7)	32
Chapter 8	Saved By Grace (Ephesians 2:8–10)	36
Chapter 9	Overcoming Divisions (Ephesians 2:11–12)	39
Chapter 10	Making One Out of Two (Ephesians 2:13–18)	43
Chapter 11	A City, a Family, a Building (Ephesians 2:19–22)	47
Chapter 12	The Mystery of Christ (Ephesians 3:1–6)	51
Chapter 13	Unsearchable Riches (Ephesians 3:7–13)	55
Chapter 14	Praying to the Father (Ephesians 3:14–19)	59

Chapter 15	In Heavenly Love Abiding (Ephesians 3:19–21)	63
Chapter 16	Christian Unity (Ephesians 4:1–6)	66
Chapter 17	Gifts for the Church (Ephesians 4:7–11)	69
Chapter 18	Preachers Who Train Ministers (Ephesians 4:11–13a)	72
Chapter 19	The Future of the Church (Ephesians 4:13b–16)	76
Chapter 20	Hating the Past (Ephesians 4:17–19)	79
Chapter 21	Becoming New People (Ephesians 4:20–24)	82
Chapter 22	Working Out the Details (Ephesians 4:25–30)	86
Chapter 23	Kindness (Ephesians 4:31–5:2)	89
Chapter 24	Inheritance in the Kingdom (Ephesians 5:3–7)	92
Chapter 25	Walking in the Light (Ephesians 5:7–12)	96
Chapter 26	Using the Time Wisely (Ephesians 5:13–17)	99
Chapter 27	Becoming Full of the Holy Spirit (Ephesians 5:18–21)	103
Chapter 28	Wives and Husbands (Ephesians 5:22–26)	106
Chapter 29	Christ and His Church (Ephesians 5:26–33)	110
Chapter 30	Relationships in the Lord (Ephesians 6:1–9)	113
Chapter 31	Spiritual Warfare (Ephesians 6:10–13)	116
Chapter 32	The Christian's Armour (Ephesians 6:14–17)	119
Chapter 33	Last Words (Ephesians 6:18–24)	123
	Some Further Reading	127

Author's Preface

The first time I preached through Ephesians was in Lusaka Baptist Church, starting on 16th April 1974 and ending on 17th July 1977. It involved about eighty messages – but not all at one time! Most of it was taken in the Evening Bible School, but then I recall I took various sub-series in the Sunday evening services. Not every preacher can sustain interest in a long string of sermons, at one place, in one series, with the same people. Most preachers do well to keep their series of sermons short – although I have to say I have not always taken my own advice! If they tackle a massive exposition, it ought to be broken up into small sub-series. Even Martyn Lloyd-Jones who was famous for preaching through Romans for fourteen years, only preached on Romans for about thirty-six Fridays of the year. The rest of the year the people had a break! And in his eight-year exposition of Ephesians, he turned aside to preach on Revival at one stage, and also took a three month break from Ephesians every year during the summer. Most pastors who try the Lloyd-Jones method will drive their congregations away, unless they have been put in a very exceptional ministry! I recall one pastor who tried it. The people liked their pastor but he went on too long and the people got to almost hate Ephesians!

I had another attempt at preaching through Ephesians in Nairobi Baptist Church, at the 8.30 am 'Youth Service', during 1980–1981, in forty-four sessions (again broken up into sections with other preachers in-between). A third major exposition began on Sunday 2nd September 1990 in 'Nairobi Cinema' which was hired by Chrisco Fellowship as one of its meeting places during that time. I lost count of how many messages there were! I finished at the end of 1991 – but it was not a case of Ephesians every Sunday. I have not preached on Ephesians in so thorough a way since then; these chapters are a rather briefer version that I have been preaching more recently in Singapore, in India, and in West Kenya.

Ephesians and Romans were the two books of the Bible that I began to ponder more than any others in my teenage years. My copy of Haldane's *Romans* has my boyhood scribbles in the margin, and I was in my teens when Dr Martyn Lloyd-Jones' *Ephesians* began to appear sermon-a-month in the *Westminster Record*. I had four volumes of *Records* privately bound before the first of the expositions were published as books. The *Records* also included sermons not available in the published volumes. Ephesians is so concentrated in its contents that this little book of mine can be no more than a hurried over-view and appetiser to the larger expositions. It is almost ridiculous to try to expound such a mighty letter in such a short space. All I can do is give a brief overview which might function as the agenda – the barest headings – for a lifetime's meditation. Dr Lloyd-Jones' eight volumes are recommended, especially on Ephesians 2 (*The Word of Reconciliation*), where he was at his best.

As I have said before on many occasions: many thanks to the Eaton and Gysling families (Jenny, Tina and Roger, Calvin, Carey, Trevecca) who take care of different aspects of my life in a way that leaves me free to write. Many thanks too to friends in the Chrisco Fellowship of Churches in Kenya, and in Chrisco Central Church, Nairobi, where I am to be found for nine months of the year and which is the place I call 'home'. Their encouragement means a lot to me. I owe a special thank you to Jane Wangechi, of Chrisco Central Church, and to Tim Pettingale and Chris Mungeam of Sovereign World publishers.

Michael Eaton
Nairobi

Chapter 1

The Greatness of Salvation
(Ephesians 1:1–14)

'Ephesians' is one of the greatest of the New Testament letters. It is not so 'controversial' a letter as many of Paul's letters. Of course the material is controversial, but what I mean is that most of Paul's letters are written to deal with serious heresies or with major failures in Paul's churches. Ephesians is written in a more positive manner and does not seem to be intended to put down any heresy or handle any opponents in any obvious manner. Romans is like this also, to a large extent. This is why Romans and Ephesians are often thought to be Paul's greatest letters.

'Ephesians' was one of the 'prison letters' written (like Philippians, Colossians and Philemon) while Paul was in prison in Rome during the AD 60s. It is quite likely that it was intended as a circular letter, to be sent to more than one church.

The letter deals with the greatness of salvation and God's plan to put everything under the headship of the Lord Jesus Christ. Paul wants his readers to see the exceeding greatness of God's power in creating the church out of both Jewish and gentile peoples (see 1:18–19; 3:8, 18, 19, 20, all of which emphasise the greatness of what God has done for us in Christ).

The main sections may be presented as follows.

1:1–2   Introduction
1:3–14   A burst of praise: the greatness of
           salvation.

1:15–19a   He begins his prayer that we might see the greatness of salvation.

1:19b–2:22   His exposition of the power of God. How we see God's power in Christ (1:19b–23), in the individual (2:1–10) and in the church (2:11–22).

3:1–13   He restarts his prayer (3:1) and then digresses to talk about how he himself has a place in God's plan.

3:14–21   He completes his prayer.

4:1–16   They must put the gospel into practice in their lives. In agreement with God's mighty plan, the first matter he deals with is the unity of the fellowship in the church.

4:17–24   He calls them to holiness in general terms. He deals with what they must not be (4:17–19) and what they should be (4:20–24).

4:25–5:7   He deals with the details of the call to godliness. Truth (4:25), anger (4:26–27), stealing (4:28), talk (4:29–30), kindness (4:31–5:2), common sins (5:3–7).

5:8–21   Two other ways of appealing for godly living. They must be light (5:8–14) and they must be full of the Holy Spirit (5:15–21).

5:22–6:9   Three sets of relationships, husbands and wives (5:22–33), parents and children (6:1–4), servants and employers (6:5–9).

6:10–20   The devil and the Christian's armour.

6:21–24   Conclusion

The first two verses are Paul's introduction. *'Paul, an apostle of Christ Jesus by the will of God. To God's holy people living in Ephesus, people who are believers, and are in Christ Jesus* (1:1). *Grace to you and peace from God our Father and the Lord Jesus Christ'* (1:2).

Paul is an apostle, one who has supreme authority to represent Jesus Christ. The first generation of apostles were literally eye-witnesses of the resurrection, and were enabled to write the word of God with a word-by-word inspiration.

Paul knows that he is writing to Christian people, people who are 'saints', 'believers' and people who are 'in Christ'.

He takes it that his readers are open to fresh blessings from God. Our great needs are 'grace' (undeserved help from God) and 'peace' (the joy of reconciliation with God). Such blessings come as we have fellowship with the Father and with the Son.

Paul's first main paragraph is in 1:3–14. He begins with a burst of praise, worshipping God for the greatness of salvation.

'Blessed be the God and Father of our Lord Jesus Christ, who has blessed us in Christ with every spiritual blessing, in the heavenly places' (1:3).

Paul plunges into praise. His heart is full. It is not enough to hold right doctrine. Do we praise God like this? Every blessing is in Christ. God has blessed us in Christ. With Christ comes everything else we need. 'Spiritual' blessings means blessings that come to us by the Holy Spirit. 'In the heavenlies' means 'in the spiritual realm'. God saves us by transferring us to a new realm altogether (see Colossians 1:13).

Next Paul explains what he means by 'all spiritual blessings'. There are blessings of the past, the present and the future, as he explains in verses 4–14.

Verses 4–6a: God's plan before history began
'He chose us in Him before the foundation of the world that we should be holy and blameless/before Him in love. He pre-destined us to adoption as sons through Jesus Christ, for Himself, according to the good pleasure of His will, to the praise of the glory of His grace.'

Verses 6b–9: God's giving us salvation in this age
'This grace He freely gave us in the Beloved. In Him we have

redemption through His blood, the forgiveness of our tres-passes, according to the riches of His grace. He has multiplied these riches of His grace towards us with all wisdom and insight, making known to us the mystery of His will, according to His good pleasure which He purposed in Christ.'

Verses 10–14: God's plan for the future

'In His good pleasure He is planning an arrangement for the fullness of times. He has a plan to bring together all things in Christ, things in heaven and things in earth – in Him. In Him also we were allocated an inheritance, having been predestined according to the purpose of Him who works all things according to the counsel of His will, in order that we might be to the praise of His glory – we who first hoped in Christ. In Christ also, having heard the word of truth, the gospel of your salvation, and having believed in Him, you were sealed with the Holy Spirit of promise, who is the down-payment of our inheritance, until the redemption of the purchased possession, to the praise of His glory.'

We notice that these verses begin with the plan of the Father, move on to the work of Jesus, and end with the work of the Holy Spirit. The Father plans; the Son mediates; the Holy Spirit applies.

Paul wants us to see the vastness and the power of salvation. How can this happen? (i) It is partly a matter of **prayerfulness**. Paul spends a lot of time praying for the people in this letter. (ii) It is also a matter of **meditation on the apostolic teaching**. (iii) It also has a lot to do with practical **experience** in the struggle to live a godly life. But we urgently need to see the greatness and the power of what God has done for us in the Lord Jesus Christ.

Chapter 2

Chosen To Be Holy

(Ephesians 1:4–6a)

Paul begins his letter with what I can only call a burst of praise. *'Blessed be the God and Father of our Lord Jesus Christ, who has blessed us in Christ with every spiritual blessing, in the heavenly places'* (1:3). God blesses us by putting us 'in Christ'. He puts us into a new realm, a new kingdom. We are transferred so that we are 'in the heavenlies' – 'in the spiritual realm'.

Now Paul comes to explain more fully what he said in verse 3. First of all he makes the point that God's plan of salvation began before God's creation of the world.

1. **We are chosen for holiness**. *'He chose us in Him before the foundation of the world that we should be holy and blameless* (1:4) *before Him in love'* (1:5a).

Predestination is a great mystery. I make no claim to understand it. But one thing is sure. There really is such a thing as God's predestination working in the lives of God's people.

Salvation did not begin from anything in us. Paul's point in saying that God's plan is 'before the foundation of the world' is to make it clear that God's plan was not based on anything we did. Before we had done anything good or bad, God was deciding to have a people for Himself. He determined to get them to be separate and distinct in the way in which they lived.

God never had any plans for us except in connection with Jesus. We are chosen 'in Him'. Christ is chosen by God as well. He is God's elect One, precious to Him (see 1 Peter 2:4). We were always chosen in relationship to Him.

This plan of God revolves around getting a people to be holy. Paul uses four phrases. (i) 'Holy' – separate, positively consecrated to God, (ii) 'Blameless' – being honest and sincere in every area of our life so that people cannot easily criticise us, and we are enjoying the approval of God, (iii) 'Before him'. Holiness is largely a matter of being conscious that God is watching us. (iv) 'In love'. This phrase could go with verse 5 ('In love He predestined us...') but I think more likely belongs with verse 4 ('blameless before him in love').

2. **We are chosen for sonship**. *'He predestined us to adoption as sons through Jesus Christ, for Himself, according to the good pleasure of His will* (1:5b), *to the praise of the glory of His grace'* (1:6a).

It was not only servanthood that was God's plan for us (although that is one way of putting the matter). It was also sonship. Once we were not God's children, but there came a time in our life when God's purpose for us was fulfilled and we were adopted as His sons and daughters. Think of the privileges of sonship. Constant access to our Father. Provision and protection. The Holy Spirit's giving us a consciousness of sonship, the Spirit of adoption. Representation. In biblical thinking a son is a representation and representative of a father. We are chosen as God's companions before we are chosen to be God's servants. God makes us His sons and daughters 'for Himself'. God wants companions. He chose us 'for Himself'.

Paul says again that this spiritual adoption came 'through Jesus Christ'. Paul will not let us forget this. He comes back to it again and again.

God's salvation arises purely out of God's own wishes. It is 'according to the good pleasure of His will'. It is not deserved by us. He loves us because He loves us (as Deuteronomy 7:7–8 puts it when referring to the nation of Israel).

3. **We are chosen for worship**. God does all of this 'to the praise of the glory of His grace' (1:6a). God especially wants us to see His graciousness. There are many aspects to God's character: His power, His anger against sin, His all-sufficiency. But we are not chosen to adoption as sons to the praise of the glory of His power, or to the praise of the glory of His holiness. What God wants us to see – more than anything – is His grace. The Bible never speaks of the treasures of God's power; it does speak of the marvellous treasures of His grace. God want our praise and our worship because we have experienced His grace.

Why does Paul want to tell us about this 'predestination' of God? Because if God has determined that I should be holy then there is some encouragement for me. If God is determined to do this, then I can be confident it is going to happen. If God has resolved before the foundation of the world that I am going to be conformed to His Son, our Lord Jesus Christ, then I have reason to believe that He is going to do what He has determined to do.

If God has decided that I am going to be His child 'according to the good pleasure of His will' and not 'according to the good pleasure of my will' then I can be sure that God is going to go on working in this way in my life. It is His good pleasure. It is what He wants to do. It is not dependent on how good and clever I am. All I have to do is co-operate with Him and He is determined to achieve His purposes in my life.

If back behind my salvation are certain things that God is determined to do with me, then I may start praising the glory of His grace now! The image of God's Son is to appear in me. God has predestined it. All of His mighty power is set upon fulfilling His purpose in my life. If this is what we are chosen to be, we may as well start co-operating with Him straightaway.

17

Chapter 3

A Mighty Plan

(Ephesians 1:6b–10)

In the middle of verse 6 Paul moves from the distant past to the present. God predestined us to the praise of the glory of His grace, said Paul. Now Paul turns to what God has done more recently, to what we are experiencing now. He says, *'This grace He freely gave us in the Beloved'* (1:6b).

1. **God gives us grace in great abundance**. 'This grace He freely gave us in the Beloved...'. Paul uses a word that means to give lavishly, abundantly, graciously. God's plan for me and for all His people was put together before creation, but there comes a time in my life when God pours out this abundant grace upon me. It is 'grace upon grace' (John 1:16). It is grace that rules and reigns in abundance where once sin was present in abundance.

God's grace comes to me because of what God thinks about His Son. It comes 'in the Beloved'. God loves His Son. And God's salvation consists of getting me to be 'in Christ'. One reason why God pours out an abundance of grace upon me, is that He views me as His beloved one just as He viewed Jesus as His 'Beloved One'.

2. **God's grace comes to us in 'redemption'**. Paul says: *'In Him we have redemption through His blood, the forgiveness of our trespasses, according to the riches of His grace* (1:7). 'Redemption' is the release of a slave or of a person condemned to death, by the payment of a price. Israel had to be redeemed from slavery in Egypt by the death of the lamb. In the Mosaic law sometimes a person might be

'redeemed' from the death penalty by the payment of a price. In Paul's day in the cities of the ancient world slaves would sometimes be released if a price for their release was paid. This was called 'redeeming' the slave.

God redeems us by the price-paying of the blood of His Son. Jesus' death upon the cross was what it cost God. It was the price that paid for our sin, and got us freedom and release. It might be asked: who was the price paid to? The Bible does not press the picture-language to ask this question, but if it has to be answered the answer would be 'to His own holiness'. God Himself determined that sin would receive its penalty, but He sent the penalty upon His Son. We were redeemed, bought at great price, to be given perfect freedom in serving God.

The greatest aspect of this release is the forgiveness of sins. God forgives all my sins when I put trust in the blood of His Son.

Again Paul lets us know that this graciousness is poured upon us richly, overwhelmingly, amazingly. 'In Him we have redemption ... according to the riches of His grace'. God's ways of grace surpass our understanding.

3. **God's grace brings us in to be involved in His whole plan of salvation**. Paul speaks of 'the riches of His grace (1:7b), which He has multiplied towards us with all wisdom and insight' (1:8). Or we could translate it as a new sentence. *'He has multiplied these riches of His grace towards us with all wisdom and insight* (1:8), *making known to us the mystery of His will, according to His good pleasure which He purposed in Christ* (1:9). *In His good pleasure He is planning an arrangement for the fullness of times. He has a plan to bring together all things in Christ, things in heaven and things in earth – in Him!'* (1:10).

Since men and women have fallen into sin, the entire universe has been falling apart. Men and women are hateful towards each other. God and man are mutual enemies. Creation does not easily submit itself to human shepherding. Angels and men have no fellowship. Tribes and nationalities are full of bitterness and rivalry. Fragmentation rules the world.

God's plan is to bring it all back together again and put it under Christ! He brings us into His plan. He has multiplied these riches of His grace towards us with all wisdom and insight, making known to us the mystery of His will. He wants us to be involved in His purpose. It starts by our being right with God. Then we help others to be right with God. We reconcile tribe and tribe, nation and nation, by bringing people to a knowledge of the Lord Jesus Christ. God goes on doing this all the time, and we do it with Him. It is not a matter of bringing unity by political discussion, or by clever organisation. It is done – says Paul – in and through this redemption which is in the Lord Jesus Christ. God is working His way towards a goal. God is getting His church to be this new human race, gathered into a unity under the Lord Jesus Christ. It is this point that Paul will take up again and again, later in his letter. Ephesians 2:11–22 and 4:1–16 pursue this matter that Paul mentions here for the first time.

God's plan is a matter of His 'good pleasure. He makes known to us the mystery of His will, 'according to His good pleasure' – just because this is what He wants to do. Paul tells the Ephesians all of these things in order that they might co-operate with God's plan. Sin fragmented our world. Jesus is building a new world by bringing people to unity under Himself – and He wants us to co-operate in what He is doing. In Ephesians 2 and 4, Paul will develop the point. God's plan involves overcoming or abolishing temporary or sinful barriers among men and women. It involves creating 'one new man', the church of Jesus Christ. It involves maintaining unity amidst the great variety of gifts within the body of Christ, the church. It involves us setting our sights on 'the fullness of the times', the day when all fragmentation will end. God wants a world of 'redeemed' people. He wants every nation to hear about this plan of salvation in Jesus Christ. He wants all who trust in Christ,

God's Son, to grow up into the unity of the faith. His abounding grace consists of bringing me and all the redeemed people of God into this mighty unifying plan. He gives us wisdom and insight to see what He is doing, and to see what we are to be doing under Him. This too is part of God's abounding grace.

Chapter 4

Inheritance

(Ephesians 1:11–14)

At the end of verse 10 Paul moved from the present to the future. God has a plan for the future, a plan 'to bring together all things in Christ'. Now he speaks of our part in that plan.

God starts this work of reuniting the universe – says Paul – by bringing into being a united human race under Christ. Paul refers first to Jewish Christians ('we who first hoped in Christ') and then goes on to mention the Ephesians who were gentile Christians ('you also'). In this passage 'we' means the earliest generation of Jewish Christians; 'you' means 'you gentile Christians at Ephesus'.

First, **he has something to say about Jewish Christians**. *'In Him also we were allocated an inheritance, having been predestined according to the purpose of Him who works all things according to the counsel of His will* (1:11), *in order that we might be to the praise of His glory, we who first hoped in Christ'* (1:12).

1. **Christians are allocated an inheritance**. The translation here is disputed. (i) Sometimes it is taken to mean 'we were chosen' (see the New International Version – NIV). (ii) Sometimes it is taken to mean that we were 'made an inheritance' for God. The idea that God has believers as His inheritance is sometimes found in the Bible. (iii) Sometimes it is taken to mean that we have already obtained our inheritance; 'we have obtained an inheritance' says the old Authorised Version. The first interpretation makes Paul

repetitive; it twice has the idea of being chosen. The second interpretation is good biblical thinking but has no parallel in Ephesians. The third interpretation gives the impression that inheritance is automatically received with our initial salvation; this is out of harmony with Paul's teaching elsewhere.

The most likely translation is: 'we were given an inheritance' or 'we were made heirs' (see NIV footnote) – that is, people who will get an inheritance. I translate: *'we were allocated an inheritance'*. It is common biblical teaching that believers will 'inherit' the promises. They must persist in faith so as to get to their inheritance. Paul often mentions it after he has mentioned justification or sonship (as in Romans 8:16–17) and it seems he does the same here. He mentions the matter explicitly in 1:18.

2. **The pathway of our life is also planned**. We are allocated an inheritance, 'being predestined according to the purpose of Him who works all things according to the counsel of His will...'. This means that not only is our actual future inheritance planned for us; also God has planned the course that we shall take in life to get to our inheritance. Our good works are foreordained (as Paul will say in 2:10). God is working everything together in our life so as to bring us to our destiny.

3. **Our fulfilling our destiny will bring glory to God**. When we achieve God's will for our life it will be 'to the praise of His glory'. We shall get honour for achieving something of God's purpose, and He will get honour too.

Next, **Paul tells us that gentiles will be involved in this also**. In verses 11–12 Paul is speaking of 'we who first hoped in Christ', the first Christians who were all Jews. But now he says that gentile believers are destined for inheritance also (see what he will say in 3:6). He says, *'In Christ also, having heard the word of truth, the gospel of your salvation, and having believed in Him, you were sealed with the Holy Spirit of promise* (1:13), *who is the down-payment of our inheritance until the redemption of the possession, to the praise of His glory'* (1:14). The same salvation and inheritance that has come to Christian Jews has also come to Christian gentiles. The proof that Christian Jews and Christian gentiles are equal at this point it that gentiles have received the Holy Spirit just as Christian Jews have.

After a person has heard the gospel and has trusted Jesus Christ, he can expect to receive the 'seal' of the Holy Spirit. We remember the story of Acts 10 and 11. When the gentiles first came into the church it was perfectly clear that God had accepted gentile believers because He gave them the outpouring of the Holy Spirit. Acts 10:44–47 and 11:15–18 are parallel passages to Ephesians 1:13.

This gift of the Spirit is obviously a conscious experience. Paul is referring to more than a secret and hidden new birth. (i) It was an obviously experiential matter in Acts 10 and 11. (ii) Paul goes on to say that the seal of the Spirit is a down-payment of our inheritance; and it is not possible to have a down-payment of heavenly glory without knowing about it. (iii) Similarly in Galatians 3:1–5 Paul refers to a gift of the Spirit which follows simple faith. Paul was looking back to something that was well-known in their experience. (iv) How can a 'seal' be secret and hidden? A 'seal' is that which makes things certain and obvious. The outpouring of the Spirit is obvious to others (as in Acts 10:44, 45) and it is surely obvious to the persons themselves (see Romans 8:15–17 which has much in common with this passage).

The sealing of the Spirit is a foretaste of heavenly reward. You were sealed with the Holy Spirit of promise, says Paul, *'who is the down-payment of our inheritance until the redemption of the possession, to the praise of His glory'* (1:14). The sealing of the Spirit is a down-payment of heavenly reward. It is a part of heavenly joy, empowerment and assurance that will be fully given to us in heaven. Paul says it is a down-payment until we get our full reward on the day when our final redemption comes to us, that is, on the day of resurrection.

The sealing of the Spirit should motivate us to go after our final inheritance, because it is the foretaste of our final inheritance. The 'sealing' is an experience now of what we shall have in great abundance in heavenly glory. The person 'saved through fire' loses inheritance. The person 'rewarded' receives a high level of glory. The 'down-payment' of the Spirit is a sample of the reward he is looking for.

Chapter 5

Opened Eyes

(Ephesians 1:15–19a)

Paul has given his survey of 'all spiritual blessings' that come to us in and through the Lord Jesus Christ. Now from 1:15 to 3:1 he will be seeking to explain more fully what he means. He will be speaking more of the power of God, the inheritance that comes to Christians, Jewish and gentile, and their equality in the Lord Jesus Christ. In 1:15 he turns from praising (see 1:3) to praying.

Paul's great desire for the Ephesians is that they may see the greatness of what has happened to them in Christ. They are part of a massive and vast plan of God to unite every-thing in the universe under the headship of the Lord Jesus Christ.

Paul turns to prayer for these Ephesians. It is not enough for a Christian teacher or apostle to teach people. He must pray for them as well. *'For this reason, I for my part, having heard of your faith in the Lord Jesus and the love which you have towards all the saints* (1:15), *do not cease to give thanks for you, when I make mention of you in my prayers'* (1:16). The two outstanding marks of the Christian are faith and love. The Christian life begins with faith and it expresses itself in love. Paul has heard that the people in and around Ephesus have become strong Christians. (Paul's words here confirm that 'Ephesians' is some kind of circular letter. Paul is obviously writing to a wider circle than to his old friends of Acts 20:17–38.) They have firm faith; they are expressing their faith in love towards each other. But to faith and love must be added hope – expectation of what God is going to do for them in their future. Paul is praying that they may go on to the next stage of Christian maturity.

People who have already come to salvation still need further enlightenment. Although Paul knows his friends in Ephesus are Christian people, he wants God to do much more for them. *'I am asking that the God of our Lord Jesus Christ, the Father of glory, may give to you the Spirit of wisdom and of revelation in the knowledge of Christ* (1:17). *I pray that the eyes of your heart may be enlightened in order that you may know what is the hope of His calling, what are the riches of the glory of His inheritance among the saints* (1:18), *and what is the exceeding greatness of His power towards us who believe'* (1:19a).

We tend not to see the greatness of God's salvation. We need teaching, and Paul is about to give them great teaching in this matter. But teaching is not enough; he is also praying for them. His prayer for them is also a suggestion of what they ought to be praying for themselves. There are three things he is asking for them.

1. He wants them to see **the hope of His calling**. 'Calling' is God's work of bringing us to Christ. Paul knows that these Ephesian Christians have been called into fellowship with Jesus. Now he wants them to be people of 'hope' as well. The word 'hope' does not refer to any kind of **doubtful** desire that maybe something will happen. We sometimes use the word that way. 'I hope to visit my parents', we say. We mean it might be possible, it might not. But that is not the way the word is used in the Bible. It does not mean 'hope' in that sense. It means expectation, anticipation, looking forward to something we know will come. Every Christian needs to be gripped with the conviction that God is putting everything under the headship of the Lord Jesus Christ, and that we ourselves have a share in this plan of God. In general we all have the same expectation – the hope of sharing in the glory of Christ. But in detail we shall all have a different route to follow, different things in detail to achieve for God.

2. He wants them to see **what are the riches of the glory of His inheritance among the saints**. God has an inheritance for us. People who are already Christians need to have their eyes enlightened to see more! What they need especially to see is the greatness of their inheritance. What is our inheritance? May the Holy Spirit open our eyes to see the answer! It begins in this life. It is heavenly reward being given to us even now. It is the presence of God. It is reaping eternal life back from the Spirit. It is being 'filled' with God's joyful energy (Matthew 5:6).

3. He wants them to see **what is the exceeding greatness of His power towards us who believe** (1:19a). This is the matter about which he will say the most. It will be the theme of the rest of the chapter and of Ephesians chapter 2. It will be the theme of his prayer in Ephesians 3:20–21.

This is what we ought to pray for ourselves. We need to ponder and meditate on Paul's teaching, verse by verse, line by line, word by word. Then we need the Holy Spirit to open the eyes of our heart that we may see God's great power working on our behalf.

This is not the kind of thing that is given in a few minutes' prayer at the end of a meeting. This requires not a few minutes of prayer and meditation but a whole lifetime of prayer and meditation. Every day of our lives we need to be asking God to show us these things by His Holy Spirit. The grace of God is much greater than we realise. Our future expectation is staggeringly great. The exceeding greatness of God's power is at work in our lives. The Christian life is not just a matter of our 'making a decision'. It is a powerful change in our entire nature and character. It is the mighty power of God bringing about a change in our lives. And that exceedingly great power continues to work in us. Our eyes need to be opened to see it.

Chapter 6

The Power of the Resurrection

(Ephesians 1:19b–23)

Paul now wants to explain what he means by the 'exceeding greatness of God's power'. He has three ways of doing it. He will show God's power in the resurrection of Christ (1:19b–23), in the spiritual resurrection of the Christian (2:1–10), and in the creation of the church (2:11–22).

1. **You see the exceeding greatness of God's power in what Christ has been raised from**. The resurrection of Jesus was the greatest demonstration of the power of God. Paul says: *'This power is in accordance with the working of his mighty strength (1:19b) which He accomplished in Christ when He raised Him from the dead and seated Him at His right hand in the heavenly places (1:20), far above all rule and authority and power and dominion, and above every name that is named, not only in this age but also in the age which is to come' (1:21).*

Death itself is a mighty power. 'The cords of death entangled me' said the Psalmist (see fully in Psalm 18:4–5). Death has rights over us, because it is the salary paid by sin (Romans 3:23). Death dragged even Christ down to its depths. But God has greater power!

2. **You see the exceeding greatness of God's power in what Christ has been raised to**. God did not only overcome death. And He did not only bring Jesus back to where He was before. He took Jesus higher and higher until He was King of the universe. He is at the Father's right hand. That is, He executes the Father's will. He is above every conceivable

power, every thing that you can put a name to. He is seated because His work of atoning for sin is finished. He now is enthroned and reigns in heaven, bringing about the Father's will.

3. **You see the exceeding greatness of God's power in the demonic powers Christ has conquered**. He is above 'all rule and authority and power and dominion, and above every name that is named'. These terms refer to various kind of opposition that attacks God and His people.

4. **This exceeding greatness of God's power is at work on behalf of God's people. Paul says,** *'And God put all things under His feet, and appointed Him to be the head over all things for the church* (1:22) *which is His body, the fullness of Him who fills all in all'* (1:23). Jesus has defeated every enemy that might be against us. All circumstances, all the powers of sin, everything is defeated by Jesus. He reigns for His church, to enable His church to share with Him what He is doing for the rest of world-history.

5. **The power of Jesus flows into His church**. The church is His body. It is joined on to Him with all of His life and energy given to the body. Just as a body shares life and energy and blood and breath, so all the people of God share Jesus' heavenly, resurrection-power.

The church is 'the fullness of Him who fills all in all'. 'Fullness' means 'that which makes something complete'. This is mysterious teaching. The idea is that the church is a kind of extension of Jesus. Jesus is not here in His literal earthly body. The church is His body! Of course Jesus is never incomplete in Himself. But in a sense Jesus needs the church. What is the use of a head without a body? What is the use of a husband without a bride. Jesus needs His church. He has organised things such that the church is His 'completion', the one by which He extends Himself to work in this world.

The church is joined on to Jesus. The church is in **union** with Jesus. It is like a body with its limbs. It is like the 'one flesh' relationship between husband and wife. It is like the joining of branches on to a tree. The power of Jesus flows into the church.

This is the secret of the Christian life and the secret of church-life. We learn to rely on this union with Christ. It is already there. We learn to trust Him. We believe that we can do all things because Christ empowers us moment-by-moment with His resurrection power. We are strong 'in' the Lord. We have a connection with the head (as Colossians 2:19 puts it). He is the vine; we are the branches. We are the wife; He is the husband who leads us, guides us, provides for us, cares for us, empowers us.

All of this should affect the way in which we think about the church. The church is not some mighty human organisation. Nor is it just a fleet of little congregations all doing their own thing. The church is the body of Christ, the body through which Jesus gets things done in this world.

Jesus 'fills all in all'. It means that He has a position of power in all respects in every part of the universe. The one who has power over everything in every way puts forward that power in and through the church.

We shall never understand the heart of our Lord Jesus Christ until we understand how great and important to Him is His church. He is our heavenly leader. He is leading His people through the world, through the history of the world, and on to the fulfilment of His plan for the world. The story has not ended yet. But we shall be involved in that story if we are involved with Jesus and therefore involved with His worldwide church. Our task is to see what He is doing and be used by Him in what He is doing. There is more to come. There will be a 'latter-day glory' in which the church will come to a greater level of blessing than has ever been known. Jesus is taking His people to where He wants them to be. Whatever happens in this world, we need to know that 'God put all things under His feet, and appointed Him to be the head over all things for the church'.

Chapter 7

Dead – But Made Alive

(Ephesians 2:1–7)

Paul is now explaining what he means by the exceeding greatness of God's power. It is seen first of all in the resurrection of Christ (19b–23). But next that same resurrection-power is seen in the new birth of the Christian. *'And God made you alive'*, says Paul. The same power which raised Christ from the dead, also raised Christians from their spiritual death. The same 'exceeding greatness of God's power' which was needed to raise Christ and make Him the king of the universe, that same power was needed to raise the Christian to newness of life. This shows the severity and greatness of the human problem. The Christian was not just a little bit sick, or a little bit needy. He was not a person who was basically all right but needed a bit of help. His problem was as severe as the problem of Jesus when He was dead and buried and sealed in a tomb. The Christian was also – at one time – dead and buried and sealed in a tomb. It takes resurrection-power for anyone to come to salvation at all.

Ephesians 2:1–3 analyses the depths of the human problem. *'And God made you alive, you who were dead in your trespasses and sins* (2:1), *in which you once walked, following the course of this world, following the ruler of the power of the air, the ruler of the spirit that is now at work in the sons of disobedience'* (2:2).

There are at least five aspects to the human condition without the grace of God.

1. **Men and women are spiritually dead**. 'God made you alive, you who were dead . . . '. Paul's description here is very severe, but we need to take it seriously. Unless we realise how deep is man's problem we shall grasp at superficial answers. It is not the circumstances of men and women that are wrong; it is human nature itself. By nature men and women are spiritually dead. They are insensitive, unresponsive towards God, without any longing or appetite for God. Of course, there are plenty of people who are religious and have ideas about God and even think they like God. But they are born without appetite for the God of the Bible! The idea that natural people are wanting God is not right. Men and women are dead. They are ignorant of the God and Father of our Lord Jesus Christ.

2. **Men and women follow the course of the world**. There is a kind of anti-God mentality in the world. Men and women are in the grip of this anti-God mentality until released by Christ. They like sin and selfishness, and they **corporately** like sin. There is a **collective** anti-God outlook which has power over the entire human race. You 'walked, following the course of this world' says Paul.

3. **Men and women are controlled by the devil**. Back behind the world is 'the ruler of the power of the air, the ruler of the spirit that is now at work in the sons of disobedience'. There is an evil principle working powerfully in this world. Paul calls it 'the power of the air' and 'the spirit that is now at work in the sons of disobedience'. Over this spirit or power is a ruler, a personality that the Bible elsewhere calls Satan or the devil (2:2). Every Christian was once in this state. 'Among these we all once lived . . . '.

4. **Men and women are naturally in bondage**. *'Among these we all once lived in the passions of our flesh, following the desires of body and of mind, and so we were by nature children of wrath, like the rest of mankind'* (2:3). Our very natures were in the grip of sin. This is why Paul calls unconverted people 'children of disobedience'. It means their very character is damaged and ruined and instinctively runs to disobedience.

It sets up a slavery. People are in bondage to their own desires, whether they are physical and fleshy or whether they are nice and respectable – but godless. There are the obvious desires of the flesh, but there are more subtle sins of the mind.

5. **Men and women are under God's anger against sin**. They are 'by nature children of wrath'. Everyone was in this predicament, Christians too, 'like the rest of mankind'.

A great turning point comes with the word 'But God...'. Having described the plight of men and women, Paul reminds the Ephesians how they experienced the intervention of God.

'But God who is rich in mercy, because of His great love with which He loved us (2:4) *(even when we were dead in trespasses), made us alive together with Christ (by grace you have been saved)* (2:5) *and raised us together with Him and seated us together with Him in the heavenly places in Christ Jesus* (2:6) *in order that in the coming ages He might show the exceeding riches of His grace in kindness towards us, in Christ Jesus'* (2:7).

1. **Only God's goodness beings about any change**. Any change in the plight of men and women comes about because of the great mercy of God. His graciousness, and His love are at work when anyone comes to salvation.

2. **He saved us when we were dead in trespasses**. There was no question of our coming alive **first**, and His then saving us. We were entirely impotent – dead – when God stepped into our lives.

3. **Salvation, then, is entirely and utterly from God's grace**. It is scarcely possible to put this matter in a more extreme way than what Paul says here. We did not save ourselves by our freewill or our natural ability to believe. We were dead when God did a work of spiritual-resurrection. The same power that raised Christ, saved us.

4. **Our position now is similar to that of Christ**. We are united to Him. He is alive. He is raised. He is ascended. We are made alive. A seed of new life is put into us, waking us

up to God and giving us a love towards Him. We are raised. We are ascended. Spiritually we are united with Christ in heaven!

God has a purpose in all of this: He wants to display for ever and ever the exceeding riches of His grace.

Chapter 8

Saved By Grace

(Ephesians 2:8–10)

Paul now explains what he said in 2:4–7, more from the angle of the Christian believer. He now concentrates more on the Ephesians themselves; he talks about 'you'. Ephesians 2:1–10 unfolds as follows:

- Ephesians 2:1–3 – deal with what we were.
- Ephesians 2:4–7 – deal with what God has done and what we are.
- Ephesians 2:8–10 – explain more fully how the change took place.

'*For by grace you have been saved through faith, and that not of yourselves. It is the gift of God* (2:8). *It is not of works, lest anyone should boast*' (2:9).

1. **Let us focus on some of the great words Paul uses in 1:8–9**. First: **saved**. This term is Paul's brief way of summarising everything he has referred to in verses 1–7. In verse 3 we were dead, enslaved to wicked powers, under God's anger. In verses 4–7 we see what happened to us – how we were made alive, raised with Christ, transferred to a new realm where we are seated with Christ in heavenly places. Paul now puts all this into one word: 'saved'. It means: rescued from the death of sin, rescued from the guilt of sin, the power and bondage of sin, the defilement of sin. It means: brought safely to life, to forgiveness, to a spiritual position in the heavenly realms; to spiritual power, to holiness, to total safety with Jesus.

Next: **grace**. 'By **grace** you have been saved'. Grace is the opposite of deserving something. It is God's help for the helpless, even though undeserved. We cannot be saved if wicked works get in the way. But we cannot be saved by good works either! Even faith is not a human achievement. We believe through God's grace. We do the believing, yet God is working this in us. After we have believed we give all the glory to Him, even for our faith.

The Christian is meant to have assurance of salvation. 'You have been saved' or 'You are saved'. Paul is sure about them – speaking generally. He knows they are saved. He wants them to be sure of it too. It never helps the saved person to doubt whether he is saved.

Our next word is: **faith**. 'By grace you are saved through faith'. It does not say 'by faith' but 'through faith'. Faith is the channel. It is not a human achievement. Salvation is of God. Even faith is worked in us through God's activity in our hearts. Verse 8b adds something; it goes even further. Faith is a gift of God; God works faith in us as we hear His Word (see Acts 13:48; John 6:44; 6:37; 2 Peter 1:1 which says faith is 'allotted' to us; and 1 Corinthians 12:3).

This means that any kind of boasting is excluded. Salvation is 'not of works, lest anyone should boast'. If salvation were by works you could boast. But since every aspect of our salvation comes from God, no boasting is possible. Even our first being given spiritual life (2:4) comes from God.

2. **A fuller explanation comes in verse 10**. It develops what has been said already. *'For we are His workmanship, created in Christ Jesus for good works, which God prepared beforehand that we should walk in them'* (2:10).

Salvation is God's workmanship. God is the workman. He makes us alive. He raises us. He works faith in us.

Salvation is an act of creation. Nothing creates itself. Salvation was not brought about by us. It was God's act. We did not save ourselves. God had nothing to work with. He did not use prior material. It was not because of anything in us. We were not newly created because God found something is us to re-mould. He created us anew out of nothing.

We are not saved by good works, but we are saved for good works. Our salvation is totally free. It did not come because of anything in us at all. But we still have to live a good life. This is not the cause of our salvation, but it is the purpose of our salvation. Good works do not contribute to our getting right with God. This is a bold and daring thing to say. Only the Christian faith says it! We are brought to salvation without our deserving anything. We do nothing, but we believe in Jesus Christ as the One who died upon the cross for us. And God's gift of new life becomes ours. Then – and only then – God begins to work in us in such a way that we live for Him. Then the 'good works' begin to flow in our daily living.

God has a plan for our lives. There are '... good works, which God prepared beforehand ...'. How do we get to know God's plan? We seek Him, seek to know His will. We use our gifts. God's plan will fit the way we are made. We must not be too proud; we must not be too fearful. God has a plan. Even the particular things He wants us to do are on His heart.

Although God has a plan for our lives **we are responsible to fulfil that plan**. Paul says good works are '... prepared beforehand that we should walk in them'. We have to do the walking. Because the plan is there it does not mean that we are passive and do nothing.

In all of this there is a lot that is mysterious and surprising. When we first put our trust in Christ it feels like something that we do. **We** put our faith in Jesus. **We** give our lives to Christ. Yet Ephesians 2:8–10 tells us things that we did not perhaps realise at the time we first believed. God was working in us. Even our coming to faith in Christ was actually the work of God. Our salvation was **more** by grace than we ever realised. This is why it is to the praise of the glory of His grace.

Chapter 9

Overcoming Divisions

(Ephesians 2:11–12)

We see the greatness of God's power in three ways. When God brought Jesus into the world He showed His great power (i) in the resurrection of Jesus (Ephesians 1:19b–23), (ii) in the spiritual resurrection of unsaved people (Ephesians 2:1–10), and – as we now shall see – (iii) in overcoming the hatred between different sections of the human race (Ephesians 2:11–22).

We have seen that the purpose of God in this gospel age in which we now live is to bring together all things in Christ, things in heaven and things in earth – in Him! (1:10). Men and women are hateful towards each other. God and man are mutual enemies. Tribes and nationalities are full of bitterness and rivalry. God's plan is to bring His world back together again in unity by putting it under Christ! He begins with His people. He creates united people in this world, His bride, the body of Christ, the church. Then He will bring the world under judgement and remove from the world everything that does not submit to His plan. Ephesians 2:11–22 and 4:1–16 pursue this matter that Paul mentioned back in Ephesians 1:10.

Ephesians 2:11–22 explains this third way of seeing the greatness of God's power. Ephesians 2:11–22 is the basis of Christian unity. It tells how God has broken down every kind of hostility between groups of people. This is one of the main themes of Ephesians. There are so many kinds of division among people: divisions that concern skin-colour, tribe, nationality, wealth or class, temperament, education, area of country, language. Paul begins with the greatest division of all history, the animosity between Jew and gentile.

Ephesians 2:11–22 divides as follows.

- Ephesians 2:11–12: what the Ephesians were.
- Ephesians 2:13–18: what God did for them.
- Ephesians 2:19–22: what their position is now.

The difficulty in the way of any gentiles being saved was not only that they were 'dead in trespasses and sins' (2:1–3); they were also outside of the professing people of God, the Jews. To save gentiles God not only had to deal with their sinfulness, He also had to deal with their position: outside of the people of God, and despised by the professing people of God, the Jews. There was a difference between the Jews and the gentiles, but the Jews had turned this into a barrier. There is nothing wrong with differences among people, but we should never turn a difference into a barrier.

God hates discrimination. God loves the world; He shows no discrimination. Discrimination always involves (i) pride, (ii) a blindness concerning the other person's viewpoint, (iii) a wrong sense of values – as though external matters were what counted.

Discrimination can be found amongst religious people. When people turn their convictions about God into barriers you have a terrible form of discrimination. There is only one way of overcoming discrimination – that is when both sides come to Jesus Christ.

Consider first the despised position of the gentiles (Ephesians 2:11–12).

1. **They were 'gentiles in the flesh'.** Paul says, *'So remember then that you – you who were once gentiles in the flesh, who are called Uncircumcision by what is called the Circumcision, made in the flesh by human hands – that at that time you were without Christ, being aliens from the commonwealth of Israel and strangers from the covenants of promise, having no hope and without God in the world'* (2:12).

With regard to their physical descent, the Ephesian Christians were once outside the people whom God had chosen for blessing, believers among the nation of Israel. These Ephesian Christians had been gentiles. There was a terrible hatred between Jews and gentiles. Gentiles hated the Jews as proud people. Jews thought gentiles were inferior. They despised the gentiles.

2. **They were 'called Uncircumcision by what is called the Circumcision made in the flesh by hands'.** They were sneered at by the Jews. The Jews gloried in their physical circumcision. But it was only something external.

3. **They were 'without Christ'.** Even in Old Testament times the Jewish people had 'Christ'. They did not know the name Jesus, but the Old Testament spoke of the coming Saviour. People like Abraham looked forward to the coming of Jesus. In this sense they had 'Christ'.

4. **The gentiles were 'aliens from the commonwealth of Israel'.** Israel was a community who knew something of the coming Saviour. They had many privileges. The law kept them from being as bad as they might be. God had done wonderful things in their history. They had the Word of God and the predictions of a Saviour.

5. **They were 'strangers from to covenants of promise'.** In the Old Testament God had given covenants – special promises which He swore to fulfil. They were (i) the oath which He made to Abraham to bring a Saviour out of the line of Abraham, (ii) the oath to David that the Saviour would come in his line, (iii) the promise of a new covenant which would be greater than the covenant of law that God gave Israel through Moses. The new covenant started in Israel. The gentiles knew nothing of all of this.

6. **They were 'having no hope'.** They had no hope in this life. They had no hope that their life would ever be any different. The gentiles were degraded and slaves to sin. They had no hope that God would ever come to help them. They had no hope beyond death.

7. **They were 'without God'.** God was not working in their

lives in any obvious way. They were under the wrath of God (2:3) and could not have a close relationship to Him.

8. **They were 'in the world'**. As Paul has said all sinners everywhere have an anti-God spirit, ruled by the devil (2:1–3). Israel knew something of the revelations of God's Saviour. The gentiles did not even have that but were wholly 'in the world' that was abandoned temporarily by God.

The coming of Jesus into the lives of gentiles was a staggering miracle!

Chapter 10

Making One Out of Two

(Ephesians 2:13–18)

Consider next what God did for these gentile Christians in Ephesus.

1. **God brought them near**. Paul says *'But now in Christ Jesus you who once were far off have been brought near by the blood of Christ'* (2:13). The gentiles were corporately and nationally far away from God. God brought the gospel to them, and God has done that for us too. Think of the way God brought the gospel to our country, and to the countries of the world. In many nations, He has reached out to gentiles, pagans, people who did not know God at all.

The Christian is 'brought near' to God. He or she has access to God. He is conscious of God's presence. God hears his prayers. He knows God's love for him. How can I get near to God? Not by anything I am by nature. Not by anything that is done **to** me. Not by anything I **do**. Not by Jesus' teaching. But by the blood of Christ! The blood of Christ atones for my sins. It cleanses my conscience and sanctifies my relationship to God.

2. **God brought Jews and gentiles into one body**. Paul says, *'For He Himself is our peace, who made both groups into one, and broke down the barrier of the dividing wall* (2:14). *He did this by abolishing in His flesh the enmity, which is the law consisting of commandments, expressed in ordinances, in order that in Himself He might create out of the two one new man, thus establishing peace* (2:15). *The purpose was that Christ*

*might reconcile both in one body unto God through the cross,
killing the enmity by it'* (2:16).

'He Himself is our peace' says Paul. We are not to take
this in a sentimental way. This is not a sentimental subject. It
is something strong and bold. It does not mean that God
gives us an easy life. Peace is reconciliation with God. It
then leads to peace of conscience, peace within ourselves.
It then leads to peace in our relationships.

Jesus makes peace by bringing Jews and gentiles (and all
other groups of human beings) into the one body of Christ,
the church. Paul explains how God did this.

In the case of Jews and gentiles God had to abolish His
own law, given to Israel through Moses. The biggest barrier
between Jews and gentiles was that of the law of God. The
law of Moses was given to Israel only; it was a temporary
measure. The aim of the law of God was to restrain sin.
(Law is still needed for this purpose but it does not have to
be exactly the Mosaic law.) Jesus abolished all parts of the
law of God, the ceremonies, the laws concerning holy days in
the year, the Sabbath, the laws about different kinds of
uncleanness (for example, the regulations concerning
leprosy). He abolished the food laws. Even what is often
called 'the moral law' was replaced by something higher.
(The **righteousness** of the law is still demanded by the gospel
but the way of reaching it is not by being under the Mosaic
system of law.)

In the first century temple there was a **literal** fence between
the area in which gentiles were allowed and the inner courts.
Paul uses this as an illustration of a profound spiritual
barrier. All Christians are on a level. Jewish Christians have
no advantages. By walking in the Spirit and not living under
law, all Christians are in the same position. The people of
Jesus are a new human race, consisting of people from every
section of the old human race.

At first one could get the impression that only gentiles
were far away from God and that Jews did not need
reconciling to God. It is true that Jews were near to God in

their history as a nation, yet they too needed reconciling to God, as verse 16 says. Both Jews and gentiles have to be brought into one body, and **both** have to be reconciled to God. This happened as Jewish men and women, and gentile men and women, came to faith in Christ's cross. The cross, when you put your faith in Jesus, kills enmity to God and it kills enmity among those who have believed.

3. **God arranged for the gospel-message to reach the gentiles**. Paul says, *'And He came and preached peace to you who were far away and peace to those who were near'* (2:17). It is striking that Paul says that Jesus preached to the gentile Ephesians, since we know Jesus never went to Ephesus. The thought is similar to Romans 10: Faith comes from true 'hearing'. True 'hearing' in the heart occurs when Jesus is so with the preacher that the preacher's words become Christ's words. When the early preachers went to the gentile Ephesus, Christ was preaching in them. It is the 'word of Christ' that is coming to the people. So Christ was making arrangements for the Ephesians to hear the gospel-message when Christ sent preachers to Ephesus and spoke through them.

4. **Jewish Christians and gentile Christians have equal access to God**. Paul says, *'For through Him we both have access by one Spirit to the Father'* (2:18). Prayer is coming to God and talking to Him as our Father. Prayer is a matter of coming to God as a powerful Father. We use simplicity as we pray, and are not bothered about the cleverness or beauty of our praying. We do not have to use many words. It does not matter whether we are loud or soft. We are coming to our Father.

Prayer is coming to God 'through Him', 'through Jesus'. We do not pray in the name of our worthiness, or in the name of our successes. We come to God because Jesus' blood was shed on the cross, and now is presented in heaven. Our sins were transferred to Jesus.

Prayer is to be in the power of the Spirit. The place where we pray does not matter very much. Posture does not matter very much. Prayer books are not needed. The Holy Spirit leads us to the promises of God, and encourages us once we start praying in Jesus' name.

Paul main point is: because of what Christ has done upon the cross both Jews and gentile Christians have an equal privilege of coming to God in this way.

Chapter 11

A City, a Family, a Building

(Ephesians 2:19–22)

The gentiles were aliens (2:11–12); God reconciled them to Himself and brought them into a reconstructed, law-free, Israel (2:13–18). So what is their position now? They are in the one-and-only church. Paul describes their position in the church in three ways. *'So then, you are no longer strangers and aliens, but fellow-citizens with the saints, and members of the household of God* (2:19). *You are built upon the foundation of the apostles and prophets, Christ Jesus Himself being the corner-stone* (2:20) *in whom the whole building being joined together grows into a holy temple in the Lord* (2:21), *in whom you also are built together to be a dwelling-place for God in the Spirit'* (2:22).

1. **The church is like a city-state**. Before, these gentile Ephesians had not felt at home among the people of God, and had no understanding of the national life of the people of God. But now these gentile Christians feel completely at home. With the law removed from its central position in the life of Israel, Israel has been re-formed. The Holy Spirit has been poured out on the remnant of Israel, at Jerusalem, on the Day of Pentecost. Now the gentiles have been brought into this newly restructured Israel, and even people like these gentile Ephesians became 'fellow citizens' with the first Jewish Christians. They have a new spiritual identity as God's people, and the same allegiance to Jesus that their Jewish Christian friends have. They are heirs to all that God

promised Abraham and his seed. In this new 'holy city', some are Jews, some are gentiles, but all are fellow-citizens.

2. **The church is like a family**. This picture is a deeper one. One is closer to one's family than to fellow-citizens in a city-state. God is our Father; Jesus is our elder brother. Christians are brothers and sisters to each other. We choose our friends, but brothers and sisters are people that are given to us without our choosing them. Christians **are** our brothers and sisters; it is a God-given fact. There is a deep family-unity, a family likeness among us. There are family traditions and family secrets. Even despised gentiles are full members of a highly privileged family.

3. **The church is like a building**. This is a yet deeper illustration, more profound than the previous two. For relationships in a city-state may not be close. Relationships in a family are closer, but in a building bricks and stones are built into each other. The illustration points to something even closer. Paul works out his illustration in five directions.

The foundation consists of apostles and prophets. Some believe (i) that the apostles and prophets are a unique one-generation group of men who were the channels of revelation for the first generation of the church. A once-for-all work of Christ is accompanied (on this view) by a once-for-all prophetic and apostolic revelation, including eye-witness testimony to the resurrection. (ii) At the other extreme are those who insist that apostles and their prophetic colleagues continue to the end of the age. (iii) My own view is that these two extremes must be combined. On the one hand, Ephesians 4:11–16 teaches that apostles and their prophetic colleagues must continue until the full maturity of the church. The apostles were men who founded churches. The prophets were their colleagues who spoke from God with words given by God. The first generation of apostles clearly had special responsibilities: eye-witness testimony to the literal resurrection of Jesus, the writing of the New Testament documents, the establishing by their ministry the foundation of the church. The New Testament teaching is that the **later** church is taught by the first generation. The first generation – said Jesus in Matthew 28:20 – wins the second generation, 'teaching **them** (the later converts) to observe all I have commanded **you** (the apostles and their colleagues)'. Jesus makes a similar distinction when He prays for the first generation and the later generations separately. He prays for '**those** (in later times) who will believe in me through **their** word' – the words of the group that travelled with and were trained by Jesus. This foundation of the universal church is surely 'once for all time' delivered to the saints in one generation. There may be apostles and prophets today; but today's apostles cannot contradict the first apostles! The first generation is the model for later generations. It was the first apostles who were, personally and in their teaching, the foundation of Christ's church.

The cornerstone is Christ. The church is built upon the foundation of the apostles and prophets, *'Christ Jesus Himself being the corner-stone.'* The 'cornerstone' was part of the foundation; it was the stone into which the other stones had to fit. (I reject the translation 'keystone' which was something different.) What determines whether a person is a Christian is whether he or she is 'in Christ'. No one is truly part of God's church unless he or she is united to the Lord Jesus Christ. Every true Christian has fellowship with the Lord Jesus Christ.

This holy building has a particular character. It is a building which is firm in its unity, it is a growing building; it is a holy temple.

This holy building has living stones. We Christians are the stones. There is a lot of variety in this 'holy building'. All sorts of nationalities and temperaments and characters are to be found there. They are not all oblong bricks as in most modern buildings, but the stones are of varied shapes and have to be chiselled and carved to fit well into the walls.

This holy building has a Resident. These Ephesian Christians – and we Christians of today – are 'built together to be a dwelling-place for God in the Spirit'. God dwells among us, just as He came to inhabit His tabernacle and Solomon's temple. Jesus builds His church, His temple. God comes to dwell in it. We – Jewish Christians and gentile Christians – experience Him by His Spirit.

Chapter 12

The Mystery of Christ
(Ephesians 3:1–6)

Paul was praying for the Ephesians (1:15–19a), but turned aside to speak of the exceeding greatness of God's power (1:19b–2:22). Now he **almost** comes back to his prayer. *'For this reason I, Paul, Christ's prisoner for you gentiles . . . '* (3:1). And then he digresses again! He was going to say 'For this reason I, Paul, Christ's prisoner for you gentiles . . . bow my knees before the Father . . . ' – and continue with his prayer. This is what he does say when he gets back to his thought in Ephesians 3:14. But he knows that the phrase 'prisoner for you gentiles' needs some explaining. So he turns aside in Ephesians 3:2–13 before continuing with his thought. At Ephesians 3:1 he almost returns to his prayer – but not quite!

'For this reason I, Paul, Christ's prisoner for you gentiles (3:1) – *I assume you have heard of my stewardship of the grace of God for you'* (3:2). Paul has been called by God to have a special ministry among gentile Christians. He has a 'stewardship' – a work of distributing the gospel to others. The Greek word is *oikonomia*; it is related to *oikonomos* ('steward', 'person in charge of the household', 'estate manager'). Paul used this idea as a picture of his ministry. He was an 'estate manager' responsible for distributing to others the supplies of God's kingdom. In this case, the supplies of God's kingdom is his revelation of the good news about Jesus. Paul is a steward of the mysteries of God (1 Corinthians 4:1, 2). He is entrusted with the treasures of the gospel. He has a

51

knowledge of God's plan of salvation. Other preachers have a similar responsibility (see Titus 1:7; 1 Peter 4:10, 11) but he does this work as a first-generation apostle. Paul's word 'stewardship', *oikonomia*, means 'the administration of salvation', 'the work of giving out God's gospel-supplies'. We have the word in Ephesians 1:10 and it comes again in 1 Corinthians 9:17, Colossians 1:25 and 1 Timothy 1:4.

Paul says, 'You know of course how God called me to this special work of preaching this gospel of grace to you gentiles, all over the Mediterranean world'. God raises up special people for particular ministries in the story of His church. Paul hopes that they recognise that God has given Paul this work.

'By revelation, the mystery was made known to me, as I wrote above briefly (3:3). *Looking at what I said you will be able to perceive my insight into the mystery of Christ'* (3:4). Paul is confident that as they study what he has said 'above' (that is, in Ephesians chapters 1–2), they will recognise that what he has said truly is a revelation from God. **The word of God is self-authenticating**. The Christian knows the truth of God, for himself, by the Spirit. When he reads the word of God it corresponds to what he almost knows already. 'You have an anointing ... and you all have knowledge' said John (1 John 2:20). The 'word of God is **in** you' said Paul and James (see 1 Thessalonians 2:13; James 1:21). When a person becomes a Christian 'the word' – the entire message of the gospel – takes up residence in that person's life. Within the Christian's heart there is an instinctive sensitivity to the message of the gospel. So Paul says 'you will be able to perceive my insight'. He is confident that they will recognise him as a channel of revelation to them from God. The Spirit reveals certain things, and the Bible reveals them as well. It is as if the Christian is seeing the truth twice, once by the Spirit and again in written form. The written form is stronger, clearer. When the Christian reads it under the enlightenment of the Spirit he or she sees that what is being read comes from God.

Paul continues: *'The mystery was not revealed to the sons of men in other generations as it is now revealed to the saints by His apostles and by prophets, by means of the Holy Spirit'* (3:5). What Paul is about to speak of is a revelation which had only recently (that is recently to Paul in the first century) been made specially clear. It was not totally un-revealed before, but it had never been revealed in the fullness in which it was revealed to Paul and the apostles and prophets of the first century. It is **not** true to say that the church is **not** found in the vision of the Old Testament prophets, but it became **clearer** later, in the teaching of the apostles. The Old Testament said quite clearly that gentiles would be blessed; Abraham was given that promise. Passages like Ezekiel 36, Amos 9 and Hosea 3 refer to the church (as the quotations in Acts 15 and Romans 10 make clear). But the matter became immensely clearer in the first century.

Again we notice that there are different kinds of prophets. Although apostles and their prophetic colleagues must continue until the full maturity of the church, yet the first generation gave the 'foundational' revelation to the church. It was embodied in the New Testament documents. A modern apostle does not lay a foundation working from zero; he has to lay the **same** foundation as the first-generation apostles. It was the first apostles and prophets who were, personally and in their teaching, the foundation of Christ's worldwide church. Modern apostles can only do the same thing again. They do not start from zero with their **own** doctrines.

What was this revelation that came with new clarity? *'The gentiles are fellow-heirs and fellow-members of the body, and sharers in the promise in Christ Jesus through the gospel* (3:6). What came with new clarity was the revelation that when the gentiles came into the body of Christ, the church, they would come in with full equality. The abolition of the Mosaic law, and the abolition of the special position of Israel, enabled gentile Christians to be fellow-heirs (people lined up for the inheritance God wants to give His people), fellow-members of the body, and sharers in the promises. God has an abundance of gifts He has promised to give His people. The promises are wide open to all believers, Jews and gentiles alike. It was the preaching of this revelation that was specially the work of the apostle Paul.

Chapter 13

Unsearchable Riches

(Ephesians 3:7–13)

Paul is in the process of explaining his own place in God's purpose of revealing the gospel to the gentiles.

1. **Paul's call to apostolic ministry was powerfully imposed upon him**. In no way did Paul choose himself to apostolic work. *'Of this gospel I became a servant according to the gift of God's grace given me, according to the working of His power* (3:7). He did not take the slightest step in this direction by his own choice and will. He was seized by Jesus (see Philippians 3:12) in about AD 34 at a time when he was violently opposed to the Christian church. His call to be an apostle came on the same occasion (see Acts 26:16–17). Even after his conversion Paul did not push himself swiftly into ministry among gentiles. It was not until about AD 45 that Barnabas travelled to Tarsus, found Paul, and persuaded Paul to assist the work among gentiles in Antioch (Acts 11:22–26).

To save Paul, to extract him from his previous life, to enlighten him, to give him the authority of the Holy Spirit as he spoke for Jesus, to give his words effectiveness and accompany them with signs of authenticity – it all required the working of God's power. There was nothing manipulative in any of this. Paul never pretended God's power was at work when it was not so. No deceit, no pretence was involved. He used no trickery, but simply taught the word of God plainly.

His ministry was according to the gift of God's grace. Paul was used by God as a result of God's graciousness. His gift as a preacher and apostle came through the generous spiritual enablement that come upon Paul from God.

2. **Paul's apostolic ministry combined authority with extreme humility**. On the one hand, he speaks with great authority. He has received revelations from God, and he knows it! He has a call from God in his life, and he knows it. Yet on the other hand, Paul speaks with extreme humility. *'To me, less than the least of all the saints, this grace was given to preach to gentiles the unsearchable riches of Christ* (3:8), *and to make plain to all people what is the administration of the mystery hidden for ages in God...'* Paul regards himself as totally and utterly unworthy. He knows that everything that has made him what he is has come to him entirely because of God's kindness to him.

3. **Paul marvels at the greatness and the wonders of the gospel**. What increases the sense of privilege that is in his heart is the marvel of the message itself. He preaches 'the unsearchable riches of Christ'. It is such a vast theme. One thinks of the glory of Christ Himself, His amazing combination of meekness and majesty, deity surrounded by weakness. One thinks of what flows to us from Him: wisdom, righteousness, sanctification, final glorification. We praise God for 'the treasures of wisdom and of knowledge', the clothing of His righteousness over our weaknesses, His sympathy, His being tempted at all points, His faith, His boldness, His character as a godly man, the life and energy that He puts into us, the power of His Holy Spirit, the fruit of the Spirit that He works into us, His companionship, His guidance ... The theme is 'unsearchable'; one never gets to the bottom of it, never gets to the end of it.

This grace was given to preach to gentiles the unsearchable riches of Christ (3:8). 'This grace was given ... to make plain to all people what is the administration of the mystery hidden for ages in God.' Paul was (i) opening up a treasure-store; and he was (ii) revealing an amazing mystery.

The gospel was hidden for centuries. Why did God take so long before He revealed it? One reason was to make it quite clear that men and women could never provide salvation for themselves. Salvation in Jesus Christ, God's Son, could never have been invented by any man or woman. For a start, the 'natural man' does not see the greatness of his sinfulness. He or she would never even realise such a salvation is necessary! The origins of salvation are mysterious. The precise way God brings His good news to our world, using a persecutor like Paul, using weak sinful people like you and me, is all something that never could have been imagined. The **future** of the gospel is mysterious was well. 'I do not want you to ignorant of this mystery', he says in Romans 11:25. All Israel shall be saved (11:26a).

A 'mystery' (as Paul uses the word) is something that could not naturally be known but which God has now revealed. Paul knows that his work is wonderful: to make plain to all people what is the administration of the mystery hidden for ages in God.

4. **Even the angels will marvel at the wonders of the gospel**. This gospel was *'hidden for ages in God (who created all things) (3:9) in order that now the manifold wisdom of God might be made known to the principalities and the authorities in the heavenly places through the church (3:10), according to the eternal purpose which God accomplished in Christ Jesus our Lord (3:11).*

One reason why God kept the gospel secret for a long time was to display it in all its glories to the angels. As the angels look at the church they see 'the manifold wisdom of God'. Not only does God have great knowledge; He has marvellous wisdom – skill at getting things done! The angels have been watching what God is doing, following the history of Israel, and now gazing in wonder at God's re-structured Israel, the church. This is why the church is so important. The church is God's way of displaying His wisdom to the angels (see also 1 Peter 1:12).

Paul slips in the phrase, 'who created all things'. It lets us know that God is well able to supervise what is happening in His world. The words 'in order that . . .' follow the reference to hiddenness. The point is: God hid His salvation to make His wisdom eventually more obvious.

It is God's eternal purpose to display His great wisdom. It has been on His mind since before the foundation of the world. His plan is now accomplished in Christ Jesus. It is already taking place. The function of the church is to be a screen on which the amazing varied wisdom of God is displayed.

5. **Such a gospel gives us boldness and confidence**. There are two implications in what Paul has said: (i) Such a gospel should give us boldness in prayer. *'In Him we have boldness and access with confidence through His faithfulness'* (3:12).

(ii) It should give us confidence in trouble: *'So I am asking you not to lose heart because of my sufferings on your behalf; these are your glory'* (3:13). If God has an eternal purpose to display His wisdom, they should trust God to know what He is doing when His servant Paul is in prison. Actually Paul's sufferings are 'their glory'. Sufferings they endured, sufferings which they saw illustrated in Paul, were only laying up treasure in heaven for him and for them.

Chapter 14

Praying to the Father

(Ephesians 3:14–19)

Paul now resumes and concludes the prayer that he started in 1:15–19a, and almost restarted in 3:1. He picks up where he left off.

'For this reason...' Words like these in 3:1 looked back to 1:19b–2:20. It meant: 'Because of the great privileges that you Ephesian Christians have in your complete access to God the Father'. Now as Paul repeats these words it means even more: 'Because of the greatness of the unsearchable riches which you may experience in the Lord Jesus Christ'.

'For this reason I bend my knees before the Father (3:14), *from whom the whole family in heaven and on earth receives its name* (3:15), *that He will grant you according to the riches of His glory, to be strengthened with power, through His Spirit, in the inner man'* (3:16).

1. We see **the posture he adopts in prayer**. He bows down before the Father. Our posture in prayer is not the most important thing and we are not to be superstitious about it. People can pray when bowing (Genesis 24:52) or kneeling (Acts 21:5) or prostrate on the ground (Matthew 26:39) or with bowed head (2 Chronicles 29:29). The important thing is to be not superstitious nor careless, but reverent.

2. We note **the way in which he thinks of God**. He is still thinking of what he said in Ephesians 2:18–22. Verse 14 picks up from 3:1, which itself picks up the thought from 2:18–22. At the end of chapter 2, he said that the gentile believers became 'fellow citizens with the saints'. Paul is still

thinking of this matter, when he says God is 'the Father from whom the whole family in heaven and earth receives its name'. The entire people of God in heaven and on earth are one family. Paul is not thinking of angels at this point, because he is thinking of God's being Father–Redeemer of all His people. That relationship does not include the angels. Paul is specially praying for these **gentile** Ephesians. He wants them to realise that they are not in any inferior position just because they are gentiles. There are great spiritual blessings (1:3) for all God's people and the Ephesians are in the **one** family of God just as much as anyone else. Paul wants to pray that they will enter into the treasures of the gospel but he reminds himself and them that God is their Father as well as Father to those 'who were the first to hope in Christ' (1:12). The whole family of God gets its 'name', its being and character, from the one Father.

3. So we come then to his **prayer for strength from God**. This is a preliminary request. He prays for them to have strength in order to receive certain **other** blessings that he goes on to pray for in verses 17–19. Before they can have Christ dwelling in them (in the way that he has in mind) they need strength from the Holy Spirit. Paul prays about one thing in order to move on and pray about another thing.

He prays that they might be strengthened in the inner man. Apparently they are not ready to experience the great blessing he mentions in verses 17–19. He must pray for something that gets them ready for the experience he is about to mention.

What does Paul mean by the 'inner man'? The New Testament has a whole list of terms that stress different aspects of man's personality: soul, spirit, flesh, body, heart, mind, conscience. Three places in the New Testament mention 'the inner man' (Romans 7:22; 2 Corinthians 4:16; and Ephesians 3:16). It means the inner personality. Man's body decays but the Christian has an 'inner man' that is not decaying. Peter speaks of 'the hidden person of the heart' (1 Peter 3:4). It is the centre of a person's being, his personality, her personality, that aspect of our being which continues to exist when our body is buried beneath the ground or thrown to the elements. In the Christian this 'inner man' is alive unto God, yet it is weak and needs strengthening.

What does this strengthening consist of? (i) We need a strengthening of **sensitivity** to spiritual things. We need to be constantly aware of God and His presence and what He thinks of us. (ii) We need a strengthening of **mind**, a clear realisation of what is available to us in the kingdom of God. We need 'ointment to put in our eyes' so that we can see, because we tend to be poor in the things of God and blind to what He wants to give us (see Revelation 3:17). (iii) We need a strengthening of **will**, a determined resolve to seek the presence of Jesus and find in a greater way than ever before. (iv) We need a strengthening of **spiritual appetite**, so that we desire to know Christ and the power of His resurrection. (v) We need a strengthening of inner **endurance** so that whatever we may have to work through in order to lay hold of Christ does not discourage us and cause us to leave off the pursuit of God's will. (vi) Sometimes – when the love of God is overwhelming – we even need strengthening of the **body**.

The strengthening is to be done, 'according to the riches of His glory'. When Paul speaks of 'riches' it is the merciful and gracious side of God's character that he has in mind. God is willing to richly shower His mercy upon us, in answer to Paul's praying and the Ephesians own praying for themselves. The strengthening is to be done 'through the Spirit'. It is part of His continuing ministry to us. As we ask God for strength, His Spirit comes to be the answer to our praying.

4. The next step is the heart of Paul's prayer. We are to be strengthened ready for the conscious indwelling of the Lord Jesus Christ, ready for being rooted and grounded in love, ready for comprehending the massive dimensions of the love of Christ. Paul prays 'that He will grant you ... to be strengthened ... *in order that Christ may dwell in your hearts by faith, being rooted and grounded in love* (3:17), *in order that*

you may be strengthened so as to comprehend with all the saints what is the breadth and length and depth and height (3:18), and in order that you might know the love of Christ which passes knowledge, in order that you might be filled with all the fullness of God' (3:19).

Chapter 15

In Heavenly Love Abiding
(Ephesians 3:19–21)

Paul continues his prayer for the Christians at Ephesus. We might ask: are the petitions parallel to each other, each saying the same thing in different words? Or does each petition prepare the way for the next one which refers to something greater? Certainly the strengthening is **with a view to** the indwelling of Christ and is before the indwelling. These Ephesians are Christians; they have already been sealed with the Holy Spirit. Yet Paul is praying for more. He wants them to be strengthened (i) *'in order that Christ may dwell in your hearts by faith, and you become rooted and grounded in love'* (3:17). In a sense Christ is in the heart – the inner personality – of every Christian. But Paul is praying that Jesus will 'take up residence', that He will move in and make His presence felt. It means that Christ becomes real to us as a person. The experience comes by our diligently seeking Christ in faith. More literally translated, the Greek says: 'that Christ may dwell in your hearts by faith, **being rooted and grounded in love'** (3:17). The 'being rooted and grounded in love' is what happens when Christ 'takes up residence' in our lives. I translate it: *'and you become rooted and grounded in love'* (3:17). It is not a further request, but is what happens when Christ takes up residence in our lives. Love becomes the kind of atmosphere in which we live. We love God and we love people. Our roots go down into the love of God. Our lives are built up on the foundation of the love of God.

The next petition seems not to add anything but to repeat what was said in verse 17. So it is not building on verse 17; it is parallel to verse 17. Paul restates his petition. *'My prayer is that you may be strengthened so as to comprehend with all the saints what is the breadth and length and depth and height'* (3:18). We might ask: 'breadth and length and depth and height' – of what? Of the gospel! Of the riches of the love and grace of God! Paul wants these gentile Ephesians to know this love of God 'with all the saints', that is, as much as the original Jewish Christians on the day of Pentecost. Every believer is open to knowing the love of God, gentiles included.

Then he prays: *'and that you might know the love of Christ which passes knowledge . . . '*. He wants them to know what is unknowable! It **passes** knowledge but he wants them to know the love of Christ! There is something mysterious about this love of Christ. We do not fully understand it. It cannot be easily explained to others. It partly means that we come to a deep realisation of how much Christ loves us. But then when that happens the person who knows he is loved finds it easier to love others. The Christian finds himself in an entire kingdom of God. Love to God, love from God, God's love for others. Love flows in all directions. He is rooted downward into love; he is building upward from love. Love becomes the atmosphere in which we live. When we abide in this heavenly love, we fear nothing and no one.

There is one more step. Paul says: 'The purpose of my prayer is that you may be empowered so as to comprehend . . .' (3:18) and that you might know the love of Christ which passes knowledge, *'in order that you might be filled up to the measure of all the fullness of God'* (3:19). The highest thing of all is to become God-filled people. Something of the very character of God is imparted to us. This is what will happen to us when we have bodies raised in glory, but it starts even now. The Spirit strengthens us for the Son of God to indwell us and then for the Father to fill us with His very being, such that we become God-filled people. There is no limit. We may go on being more and more full of God *'up to the measure of all the fullness of God.'*

Paul closes this section of his letter with something that is both a prayer and an encouragement. *'Now to Him who is able to do far more exceedingly above all that we ask or think, according to the power that is working in us* (3:20), *to Him be glory in the church and in Christ Jesus to all generations for ever and ever. Amen'* (3:21).

The doxology of verses 20–21 is related to the prayer of 1:15–19a; 3:1, 15–19. When he says God is 'working in us', he is thinking of the kind of spiritual experiences he has been praying for. God is able to bring us to a level of spiritual experience that transcends what we have thought or known. He is working within us already and the power that has already been at work is able to do more. To such a Saviour–God Paul wants to give honour. He wants honour to come to God 'in the church'. Paul has several times referred to the amazing fact of the church with both Jews and gentiles within its number. Nothing but the amazing power of God could raise such degraded gentiles and such proud Jews and bring them into one body where all have equal access to the Father. Honour should come to God through this amazing community of love, the worldwide church of Jesus.

This honour also comes to God 'in Christ Jesus'. Everything that has happened to save gentiles and Jews and bring them into one body with the amazing possibility of becoming God-filled people, it all has happened through Christ Jesus. The glory will go on being given to Him, 'to all generations for ever and ever'. Paul is glad that it should be that way. He adds his 'Amen'.

Chapter 16

Christian Unity

(Ephesians 4:1–6)

Ephesians 4:1 is the major turning-point in the letter. Paul has taught the Ephesians about the greatness of God's power. He has prayed that they might experience it. Now his next concern is to appeal to them to live according to this power that is within them. Paul calls them – and us – to live a godly life. In Ephesians 4:17–24 he gives a general appeal, and then in 4:25 onwards he gets to details. But before he gets to his general appeal he has a section (4:1–16) in which he appeals for Christian unity. One can see why he does this. It is because unity between Jewish and gentile Christians has been one of his main themes. It is natural and logical for him to immediately call us to live out the unity that is created by God among His people.

'I therefore the prisoner in the Lord appeal to you to live a life worthy of the calling with which you have been called...'(4:1). 'Calling' is the word Paul uses to speak of God's powerful summons that brings us to know Christ as Saviour. The word speaks of something powerful and effective. To be 'called' is to be powerfully brought to Jesus Christ by the working of the Holy Spirit in our lives. Our salvation is not just a matter of trying to reform our lives or making a decision to be different. God saves us by a powerful pulling of drawing us into His kingdom. No one can be saved without such a drawing (as John 6:44 says). The 'call' of God is His word coming to us, plus the powerful

drawing of the Holy Spirit. It is Jesus' opening our hearts (as Lydia's was opened by Jesus in Acts 16:14).

Paul says, 'If this has happened to you, then live accordingly!'. Live in a way that corresponds to what God has done in your lives. God has powerfully brought you into His kingdom. He is ruling over you in His grace. So show it! Demonstrate what has happened to you, to yourselves and to others.

Paul himself is in prison as he writes this letter. He is 'the prisoner in the Lord'. He has utterly surrendered his life to serving God no matter what it costs him. Now he asks the Ephesians to live in the same way.

The main thing on Paul's mind as he gives this appeal for godliness is the need for Christian unity. He continues: '...*with all humility and meekness, with longsuffering, forbearing one another in love* (4:2), *making every effort to keep the unity of the Spirit in the bond of peace'* (4:3). He asks for humble attitudes and determined effort to keep the unity that the Holy Spirit has given to the church. They do not have to **create** unity; God has done that. But they have to **keep** what God has given them.

Verses 4 to 6 go on to explain what God has done to create the unity which they must keep. *'There is one body and one Spirit, corresponding to the fact that you were called with one hope of your calling* (4:4). *There is one Lord, one faith, one baptism* (4:5), *one God and Father of us all, the One who is over all and through all and in all'* (4:6). Seven facts are brought before us, all of which are things that create and absolutely guarantee the unity of the church. (i) It is a fact that God has only brought into being 'one **body**'. There are not two churches for Jews or gentiles, or for rich or poor, or for black or white – or whatever. There is one body! (ii) There is one **Spirit** that brought the one body into being. (iii) This one body comes into being as people come to salvation. People come to salvation as they are called by God. There is only one calling and it gives the people of God a common destiny. There is one **hope**. There will be no compartments for Jews and gentiles in heaven – or for any other earthly distinctions of that kind. (iv) There is one **Lord** Jesus Christ in whom all true Christians have faith. (v) There is 'one **faith**', faith in the gospel of the Lord Jesus Christ. 'The faith' is not a detailed system of doctrine; there is not much unity about the lesser details of Christian teaching! The 'one' faith that creates the unity between all Christians is the fact that all true Christians have faith in the same Saviour. The 'one faith' is saving faith, justifying faith. It is believing in your heart that Jesus is Lord. This is possessed by all true Christians. It creates their unity. Those without it have no salvation.

(vi) There is one **baptism**. What kind of baptism is it that creates and guarantees unity? Not water baptism! Water-baptism has been the source of great disunity among Christians. They have differing opinions about the subjects of water-baptism (children?) and about the mode of water-baptism (immersion?). Some are muddled about the effect that water-baptism has (does it in any sense impart grace?). One cannot say that water-baptism creates and guarantees Christian unity! No, the 'baptism' that creates and guarantees Christianity is the work of the Holy Spirit 'baptising' us into the body of Christ, 'putting' us into the true church of God, the total number of the saved. That kind of baptism is the only one that creates and guarantees Christian unity as an objective fact.

(vii) There is one God who is the Father of all Christians. He rules **over** all Christians. He is found in every part of the Christian church, so He is **through** all. He is **in** all Christians.

These are the things that create Christian unity. Paul simply asks us to keep it, guard it, let nothing damage it.

Chapter 17

Gifts for the Church
(Ephesians 4:7–11)

Paul moves from protecting the **unity** of the church (4:1–6) to protecting the **variety** of the church (4:7–10). Verse 7 begins with 'But'. *'But to each one of us grace has been given, according to the measure of the gift of Christ'* (4:7). We keep the unity of the Spirit, **but** God's grace has been given in different measures to each Christian. Each Christian has a **measure** of God's grace to use in the fellowship. This means that each Christian has a different place in the fellowship. No two Christians are identical. No Christian has all spiritual gifts. No one spiritual gift is given to all Christians. We find our place in God's church by being ourselves under God, not by fitting any special mould or copying any spiritual mentor too closely. We keep the unity of the Spirit; we keep the variety of the Spirit also.

Verses 8–10 go on to speak of what it is that enables Christ to give gifts to His church. *'Therefore it says, "When He ascended on high, He led a host of prisoners captive, and He gave gifts to His people"'* (4:8).

Where does this grace of God given to each Christian come from? It comes from the Lord Jesus Christ. He – says Paul – is the fulfilment of Psalm 68:18.

Psalm 68 is the description of a procession. God is pictured as marching from Sinai to the land of Canaan. His enemies are scattered before Him as He journeys forward. *'God will arise, His enemies will be scattered'* (Psalm 68:1). Then God ascended Mount Sinai. *'With divine chariots, twenty thousand of them, thousands upon thousands, the Lord is among them on Sinai, in the holy place'* (68:17).

Then God ascended Mount Zion. *'You have gone up on high. You led away captive a procession of conquered enemies. You received gifts consisting of people, people who were once rebels, so that the Lord might dwell with them'* (as 68:18 may be translated).

One can see why Paul would use Psalm 68:18 here. It is about God making a dwelling-place, a temple on Mount Zion, Jerusalem. Through King David God takes many prisoners captive and He makes them part of Israel! He takes prisoners captive in order to dwell among them. This is exactly what Paul has been saying throughout Ephesians. God takes hold of people who are dead in trespasses and sins, and then He incorporates them into His new temple, the church. They become fellow-citizens with the saints, members of God's new Jerusalem. They become a holy temple in the Lord. God takes **gentiles** captive to make them into His servants. Jesus ascended not into the heights of Sinai, not to the heights of Zion, but into heaven. From His position in heaven as the king of His church, He takes gentiles into His new temple the church.

Paul adapts Psalm 68 ('You received gifts') and changes the wording ('You gave gifts'). It is a way of applying Psalm 68 to the New Testament situation. It is not a 'pure' quotation of Psalm 68; it in an **exposition** of Psalm 68 in the light of what happened in the ascension of Jesus and the outpouring of the Spirit. The people that He captured as gifts for Himself – many of them gentiles – He gave back to His church as gifts for the church. Verse 11 of Ephesians 4 continues: 'And it was he who **gave** the apostles, the prophets, the evangelists...'.

Paul adds a further point of exposition. *'Now this phrase "He ascended" what can it mean but that He also descended into the lower parts of the earth? (4:9). He who descended is the same One also who ascended far above all the heavens, in order that He might fill all things'* (4:10).

70

Jesus ascended into heaven, but He also descended into 'the lower parts of the earth'. What does this 'lower parts of the earth' mean? Is it a reference to His coming to planet earth as a man, 'down to the very earth' (as the New English Bible has it)? Does it refer to the depths of His suffering on the cross (as John Calvin thought), or to His burial (as the Puritan Paul Bayne thought) or to the 'return' of Christ in the outpouring of the Spirit (as various scholars have said)? I think it means 'He descended to the lowest level of the universe, the realm of the dead'. Paul divides the world into three (see Philippians 2:10, heaven ... earth ... the depths). In His ascension Jesus becomes King over every section of the world. He 'descended' and 'ascended' 'in order that He might fill **all** things'. He leaves no part of the universe unconquered. Paul has already said in Ephesians that Jesus' kingship involves the conquering of death (1:20 as a preliminary to being the head of His church (1:21–23)). The thought is the same here.

Jesus, the conqueror of death, fills the universe with His power. He is head over all things for the church. From His position a King of the universe, He gives **people** to be blessings to His church. *'And it was He who gave the apostles, the prophets, the evangelists, the pastors and teachers...'* (4:11).

Jesus gives apostles to His church. Paul is not referring here to the Twelve, but to apostles who are given **after the ascension**. There are different kinds of apostles. Paul refers here to what I call 'post-ascension apostles', people who plant churches and are used in the same way as Paul and others for reaching large areas for Christ. Only the first generation were a foundation for the **universal** church, but a very similar kind of Christian preacher is still given to the church today. He no longer is a writer of part of the New Testament as Paul was. He cannot produce new doctrines, but he can reach continents for the Lord Jesus Christ.

Chapter 18

Preachers Who Train Ministers

(Ephesians 4:11–13a)

Paul is telling us what God's gifts to the church actually consist of. *'And it was He who gave the apostles, the prophets, the evangelists, the pastors and teachers . . .'* (4:11).

First, Paul gives us, **samples of His gifts to the church**. God gives apostles, as we have seen. God gives prophets. Prophecy is **speaking for God with words given by God**. A prophet is a person who is frequently and reliably used by God in this way. There are different levels of 'prophecy'. Under the Mosaic law the prophet was the most authoritative kind of spokesman for God. He was in a word-by-word manner inspired by the Holy Spirit in the most amazing way. His words could perhaps become part of our inspired Bible. If he turned out to be a false prophet he was subject to the death penalty. Few people were prophets.

After the giving of the Holy Spirit, every one of God's people could be used in 'prophecy' – speaking with God-given words. This is the point of Acts 2:18 which quotes Joel 2:28. Obviously the kind of 'prophesying' we are to expect today is (i) **not** on a level with the Old Testament prophets. Nor (ii) do I think it is on a level with the prophets who were the colleagues of the first generation of apostles, the eye-witnesses of the resurrection. I have to say also – reluctantly – (iii) that I am not very impressed with much of what claims to be prophecy today. Scribble down notes of it (as I often do) and watch to see how reliable it turns out to be, and it is often confusing and of no value to the church at all. The 'prophets' often are self-centred and greedy for money. Yet one must not throw out the baby with the bath-water. There is a lot of messy bath-water around, but there is a baby there somewhere!

It is possible – still – to speak for God where God is giving us exactly what to say. I would not like to claim that it is 'verbal inspiration' quite like that of the Old Testament prophets and the first generation of apostles, but it comes close at times. God can even give outlines of the future. If a person really is a 'prophet' we can expect sooner or later (with no manipulation or over-claiming) powerful evidence that what he says is right. Micah prophesied boldly and said something that was difficult to believe (1 Kings 22:17); shortly after his word was confirmed in a way that no one could doubt (1 Kings 22:34–36).

The kind of 'prophet' Paul has in mind here is not the 'God-has-told-me-you-need-inner-healing' kind of prophet (although they exist). It is the kind of prophet who assists apostles and other preaching ministries in bringing the church to a high level of practical maturity. He does so not so much by **exposition** – the work of a teacher – but by a teaching-right-now-for-this-moment based on the message of the gospel and applied to God's people with challenging clarity. A teacher normally has a text. A prophet's text is often the whole message of the Bible with illumination added into what is happening right now.

It should be added that these giftings are not **sharply** differentiated. A teacher can be prophetic. A prophet can be didactic (related to teaching). Someone can be half-and-half or even different things in different places.

God gives evangelists. They are people who focus on the evangelistic message (not the 'whole counsel of God') and have gifts of exhortation, ability in the Spirit to bring about response.

God gives pastors-and-teachers. The Greek wording ties these two ministries together. Some think they are really only one ministry of pastor–teacher. I think it better to think of two ministries that are closely related. Pastors are teachers who are good with people. Teachers are pastors who are good at exposition. The two are close to each other. Pastors spend more time with people. Teachers spend more time with their Bible.

Next, Paul gives us, **the purpose of these God-given ministries**. Paul confines himself to five kinds of preacher. There are other kinds of gifts – that is, people with special callings – who are given to the church. The purpose of **these** particular people comes next. They are given *'for the perfecting of the saints for the work of ministry, for the building up of the body of Christ, until we all attain to the unity of the faith and to the unity of the knowledge of the Son of God.'*

It is important here to see that we do **not** have three parallel phrases:

- for the perfecting of the saints,
- for the work of ministry,
- for the building up of the body of Christ.

Actually the Greek word for 'for' is different and shows that the three phrases are **not** parallel. To take it as three parallel statements would imply that only preachers are 'ministers', an idea which has seriously damaged the church for centuries. There is to be no comma after 'perfecting of the saints'. It should be read:

> **for** [Greek *pros*] the perfecting of the saints **into** [Greek *eis*] the work of ministry [and that in turn leads] **into** [Greek *eis*] the building up of the body of Christ, **until** we all attain to the unity of the faith and to the unity of the knowledge of the Son of God.

Preachers are trainers! They train people for ministry. The 'ministers' are the entire company of God's people. Every Christian has some kind of 'ministry'. Preachers train them. This in turn builds up the whole people of God.

How long does this go on for? For the entire history of the church. All five preaching-ministries continue, *'until we all attain to the unity of the faith and to the unity of the knowledge of the Son of God.'* Paul is referring here to the long-term future history of the church. The church has a goal and a destiny. There is a unity of the faith already! That was the point of verse 5. Yet there is a greater unity still to come. The church is already 'one body' with 'one Spirit ... one hope ... one Lord ... one faith', and so on. Yet there is a greater unity yet to come. It comes about when there is a fuller, deeper, richer knowledge of the Lord Jesus Christ than has ever been known in the story of the church. We have not reached it, but we are on the way. The church has a glorious future.

Chapter 19

The Future of the Church

(Ephesians 4:13b–16)

Paul describes the ultimate goal of the preaching ministries (4:13b), then spells out further implications negatively (4:14) and positively (4:15–16).

1. **The goal of the five preaching ministries is the full maturity of the church**. Paul's long Greek sentence goes on: *'until we get to being a full-grown person, to the measure of . . .'* and so on. We can make it easier by starting a new sentence. *'God gives these ministries until we become a full-grown person, to the measure of the stature of the fullness of Christ'* (4:13b). The 'full-grown person' refers to the church. The church is like a person who grows from being a child to being fully developed. It is similar to Paul's well-known use of 'body' as an illustration of the worldwide church. Christ and His church make up one 'body' or (as Paul puts it here) Christ and His church make a growing person. The work of the five ministries is to bring the church to full maturity. Full maturity is likeness to the Lord Jesus Christ (*'the measure of the stature of the fullness of Christ'*) – found in the entire church. It is a dazzling vision of the church's future!

2. **Paul describes 'church maturity' negatively**. *'The purpose is that we may no longer be children tossed to and from and carried about with every wind of teaching, by human cunning, by craftiness, in the scheming of error . . .'* (4:14).

The church goes through child-like immaturity for a time. One thinks of the early history of the church. It was often

76

extraordinarily immature. The Reformation of the 16th century was certainly a major step forward in the story of the church, but the church still has a way to go before it is 'a full-grown person'. The preaching and teaching ministries are given so that the church 'no longer' remains in that state. Children are self-centred and gullible, and many in the church are self-centred and gullible also. The teachers of the church are responsible to do something about it, and bring the church to fuller maturity. How many strange teachings come into the modern church. They last a few years before being replaced by something else equally self-centred. How many scheming and crafty preachers there are in different parts of the world. Never (certainly in poorer parts of the world) has it been so profitable to have a money-making career in some 'ministry' propped up by money from some rich country. This is the very immaturity which preachers are to overcome: winds of teaching, accompanied by craftiness, in the scheming of error (4:14).

3. **Paul describes 'church maturity' positively**. The purpose of the five ministries is that the church will no longer show childlike instability, *'but speaking the truth in love, may grow up in every way into Him, who is the head, that is, Christ'* (4:15). Paul goes on to describe what this is actually like. *'From Christ the whole body, being joined and brought together by every connecting link which gives supply, makes bodily growth, according to the working in measure of each individual part, for the purpose of building itself up in love'* (4:16).

Maturity is 'speaking the truth in love'. It is the combination of boldly standing by what God has revealed plus a loving manner towards those who are not pleased with us when we obey God's truth.

Maturity is a matter of adapting speedily to what God shows us. The mature Christian is so open to the Lord Jesus Christ that in many areas of life ('in every way') he grows into Christ, that is, he moves into obedience to Christ, and fellowship with Christ.

Maturity is learning to live on energy provided by Christ. From Christ 'the whole body ... makes bodily growth'. The church learns to receive guidance and life from the Lord Jesus.

Maturity is a matter of holding together in loving unity. The whole body is joined and brought together. There are connections between different parts of the body. In the human body there are parts which are connected by ligaments. One thinks of the elbow or the knee. The connections between the different parts of the body 'give supply'. That is, life and energy, blood and nervous impulses flow down the connections in the human body. So it is also in the worldwide church. There are connecting links. The five types of ministries **are** the connecting links. The different kinds of preacher keep the different parts of the church in touch with other parts. The five ministries 'give supply'. Life and energy flow from one part of the church to another, through the 'connecting links', through the preachers of five kinds. Life comes into the church through their varied kinds of preaching.

The result is that, as the entire church is helped by a full range of ministries, it grows – in quantity and in quality, in numbers and in depth of spirituality. For the growth to take place there must be the 'working in measure of each individual part'. Each person in the church, roused and trained by the preachers (the connecting link through which life and energy comes), plays his or her part in the worldwide church. They do so 'in measure'. That is, they cannot do everything. They live for God and His church according to the 'measure' of what has been given to them (Paul repeats the thought of 4:7).

So the church grows *'for the purpose of building itself up in love'* (4:16). The kind of growth he has in mind is partly numerical, but it is also a growth in holiness, the greatest part of which is love.

Chapter 20

Hating the Past
(Ephesians 4:17–19)

Paul is dealing now with putting the gospel-message into practice and letting it influence our lives. Because this letter has a special interest in the unity between Jewish and gentile Christians he has first urged them to keep the unity of the worldwide fellowship (4:1–16). Although I said above that 'Ephesians 4:1 is the major turning-point in the letter' it is also true that Ephesians 4:1–16 had a very close connection with the theme of unity in 1:11–14, 2:11–22 and 3:6, and was (in 4:1–16) following up those passages in an appeal for the unity of the Christians. It is only now that Paul turns to a more **general** appeal for godly living. The following sections may be set out as follows.

- In 4:17–24, he calls them to holiness in general terms, negatively and positively, what they must not be (4:17–19) and what they should be (4:20–24).
- In 4:25–5:7 he deals with some details: telling the truth (4:25), anger (4:26–27), stealing (4:28), talk (4:29–30), kindness (4:31–5:2), and the common sins of the ancient world (5:3–7).

   'This therefore I say and testify in the Lord: you must no longer live as the gentiles live, in the futility of their minds' (4:17).

   As always the word 'therefore' is very significant because it signals to us the New Testament way of preaching holiness. It means 'in the light of what I have said'. The

79

New Testament way of preaching holiness is to put before us the truth of the gospel and then ask us to work out what we know and what has happened to us. The Bible has no 'ethics' for the un-saved! The nearest to it is the Mosaic law over Israel, and the appeals to the pagan consciousness (without the Mosaic law) of right and wrong – as for example in Amos 1:3–2:5. The New Testament call for godliness is addressed only to Christians. If we know the exceeding greatness of God's power (as Ephesians 1–3 has been saying we do), then Paul 'therefore' asks us to show it in newness of life. Paul 'testifies'. It is as if he is in God's law-court. God the Judge is watching. Paul is speaking God's truth before the Judge of the universe. He is in fellowship with Jesus as he writes. Paul's main point is: 'you must no longer live as the gentiles live'. A radical change must come in the lives of these Christians at Ephesus.

Then Paul goes on to say what was wrong with them before they came to salvation, as it still is what is wrong with the rest of the world. Before they had lived 'in the futility of their minds'. In this line 'the mind' refers to the whole inner attitude and disposition. It is not purely the intellect (for that is mentioned next); it is rather the **attitude**. What is wrong with the gentiles is that sin grips their entire inner life. What is needed in them is not just a little bit of information or advice. They need a new heart, a new nature, a new inner mentality. The pagan mentality is futile: there was no success in godliness, no satisfaction, no ability to cope with life and certainly no ability to cope with death. With all their philosophical debate, the end was useless. Moral filth and suicidal negativism filled the ancient pagan world, as it does those parts of the world today which are without Christ.

Verses 18–19 develop the point further. *'They are darkened in understanding, having become alienated from the life of God, through the ignorance that is in them on account of the hardness of their hearts* (4:18). *Having become insensitive they have given themselves over in loose-living, to the working of all uncleanness with covetousness'* (4:19).

1. First Paul looks at **the intellect**. 'They are darkened in understanding...'. Even very clever people are totally dim-witted when it comes to the things of God.

2. Then Paul looks at the **spiritual death** that is involved. 'They are darkened in understanding, having become alienated from the life of God...' They are no longer alive to God. Men and women were created with the life of God in them, but it was lost in the original fall of the human race. Now they are without liveliness towards God. They are like a corpse in the matter of spiritual sensitivity.

3. Thirdly, Paul mentions something even deeper, **the wickedness of the heart**. They are 'darkened' and 'alienated' 'through the ignorance that is in them, on account of the hardness of their hearts...'. It is the heart that has gone wrong. Men and women do not need just a little bit of help. Their entire inner personality is perverse. They need a new heart. Christian conversion is a matter of having a new heart, a new and right spirit created within us by God.

4. Fourthly, there are **the results in the way men and women live**. Having become 'insensitive' – a phrase that summarises the hardness and deadness he has just mentioned – they have given themselves over in loose-living to the working of all uncleanness with covetousness (4:19). Their actual lives are full of uncleanness and greed, and they do nothing to oppose or resist the wickedness within them.

Paul is mentioning all this because he is calling the Ephesians to be 'no longer' what they were before. They are to hate all this, the blindness, the deadness, the unclean-ness, the greed. They are to do a total about-turn and walk in the opposite direction. Instead of blindness they must seek illumination, instead of deadness, sensitivity to God. Instead of uncleanness, there must be purity; instead of greed, contentment. 'You must no longer live as the gentiles live'.

Chapter 21

Becoming New People

(Ephesians 4:20–24)

Paul is giving a **general** appeal for godliness. He has asked us to break free from our past way of living. Now he puts the matter positively. He has spoken of our past wickedness. Now he says, *'But you did not learn Christ in that way'* (4:20). Paul abruptly reminds them of what happened to them at their conversion. This is the way in which we help ourselves to live a godly life: we recall and remind ourselves what happened when we first came to faith in Jesus Christ. A Christian is a person who has experienced a radical change in his life. It may perhaps have been a slow procedure in his own consciousness. It may have taken place when he was very young. Not everyone remembers the precise moment of their coming to faith in Jesus. But however it happened, a radical change has taken place in every true Christian.

When we come to our first salvation we do so because we 'learn Christ'. We come to a definite knowledge that Christ is the Son of God and the Saviour. We know something about Him, but we also know Him as a person. We 'learn Christ'.

This 'learning Christ' produces a radical change in our lives. It turns us away from the darkened understanding, the alienation from God, the ignorance that was in us on account our hardness of heart. All of that changes. You did not learn Christ in that way, says Paul. What you learned was altogether different.

What happened was that we heard the voice of the Lord Jesus Christ. *'I assume that you heard Him and you were taught in Him, as the truth is in Jesus'* (4:21), says Paul. We discover the truth. It is truth that revolves around 'Jesus', the person of the Lord Jesus Christ who came into this world as a man and was known as 'Jesus'. We learned about Him and His salvation.

We also heard Him. Paul has already said: 'And He came and preached peace to you who were far away and peace to those who were near' (2:17). In the preaching of the gospel Jesus Himself draws near to us. Jesus is with the preacher so that the preacher's words become Christ's words. Christ is preaching through the preachers of the church. So it is the 'word of Christ' that is coming to us in the preaching.

We were 'taught in Him'. As we hear Jesus, we are united to Him. We are in fellowship with Him. He Himself is teaching us by the Holy Spirit.

All of this is what happens when a person comes to his or her first faith in the Lord Jesus Christ. Paul asks us to face ourselves, to realise what has happened to us. 'Don't you know who you are and what has happened to you?' says Paul. You learned the Lord Jesus Christ. He came and spoke to you. You learned about the blindness of your heart and the folly of sin, and the hatred of God against sin. Don't live in the way you used to. The Lord Jesus Christ has taught you something entirely different.

The precise way of translating the next few lines has often been disputed. There are four possibilities. (i) Are they speaking of result? 'You learned Christ *'with the result that'* you put off the old self...'. This, I believe, is mistaken, because it gives the impression that we **automatically** throw of 'old self' behaviour. (ii) Are they speaking of obligation? 'You learned Christ; *'you ought to'* put off the old self...'. This view imposes an obligation on us but does not so much emphasise the connection between what happened at our conversion and what should be happening now. (iii) Are the clauses speaking of purpose? 'You learned Christ *'in order to'* put off the old self...'. This fits the trend of thought much better. Yet I think a fourth view makes even better sense. (iv) These verses are surely telling us the content of what was learned or taught when we were first saved. I translate: *'What you were taught was: to put off the old self according to the former way of life which is corrupted and dominated by passions and deceits* (4:22). *You were taught to be renewed in the spirit of your minds* (4:23), *and to put on the new self, created to be like God in true righteousness'* (4:24).

It will help us to understand if we notice the difference between Romans 6:1–11 (on the one hand) and Ephesians 4:22–24 and Colossians 3:9, 10 (on the other hand). Romans 6 deals with **what God does to us**. He places us in Christ by the Spirit such that the 'old self' has died. The person that we once were is gone. Romans 6 is dealing with something that has happened, something God does, not something that ought to happen, not something we do.

But Ephesians 4:22–24 and Colossians 3:9–10 are different. They are dealing not with what God does to us but **what we do for God**. Romans 6 says that the Holy Spirit unites us to Christ and as a result the old self dies; he is dead and buried with Christ. But Ephesians 4 and Colossians 3 say to us: if the actual 'old self' has gone, then the behaviour of the 'old self' should go as well. It has happened in your history and your position; you are a new man. So make sure it happens in your behaviour.

It is totally wrong to think that 'the old self' is the same as 'the flesh' (the remaining 'pull' of sin). The 'old self' and 'the new self' are not different parts of our **present** identity. The 'old self' is the person we used to be under the dominion of sin. The 'new self' is the person we are now in the Lord Jesus Christ. We are never told to mortify the 'old self'. You don't kill someone who is already buried!

When Colossians 3 and Ephesians 4 deal with our putting of the 'old self', it is not referring to our position; God has already dealt with that. Rather it is dealing with our behaviour. God buries the 'old self' by bringing us into His kingdom of grace. After that we are able to throw off the 'old self' with regard to behaviour. (i) We are a new person;

(ii) so we should live like a new person. Romans 6 deals with the first half of this combination; Ephesians 4 and Colossians 3 deal with the second half.

So there are three things we learned and ought to remember that we were taught in principle even at the point where we first heard the voice of Jesus. (i) We learned: to put off the old self. Paul is thinking of the behaviour that was characteristic of the old life. It was corrupted, polluted, far removed from what God wants men and women to be. It was dominated by passions and deceits. We were taught to get rid of the remnants of that style of life. (ii) We were taught to be 'renewed in the spirit of your minds'. Our very mentality must change. We are to constantly allow God to reshape our thinking. The 'spirit' of the mind is the attitude with which we use our mind; it is the principle that governs our thinking. We think in a new way. We bring God and His kingdom into our thinking. (iii) We put on the new self, created to be like God in true righteousness. We are already new people! But we put on the new self. If means we put into practice what God has done. God has re-created us; we have become new people. A hunger for righteousness is already in our lives. We work out what we believe and turn it into practical living. We live the life of love. We follow the kind of things Paul is about to say in Ephesians 4:25–5:7 – which really is all about 'putting on the new self'.

Chapter 22

Working Out the Details

(Ephesians 4:25–30)

Paul is still dealing with the actual living of the Christian life. He has told what our lives should **not** be like (4:17–19) and what our lives **should** be like (4:20–24). Now he gets down to details. He concentrates on six particular details.

1. **Telling the truth**. The Christian life begins with large sweeping principles, but eventually everyone has to get down to the details. Paul gets more and more practical as he goes along. He begins with being predestined before the foundation of the world (Ephesians 1:4), but eventually he gets to telling the truth and not getting angry (4:25–27). He begins in such heights but then gets down to practicalities. Yet the great heights help the practical details. *'Therefore putting away lying, speak the truth each one with his neighbour, for we are members of one another'* (4:25). He asks us to speak the truth. This is something that a lot of thinkers and philosophers ask of us also. But the important thing to notice is that Paul gives **Christian** reasons for what he says: 'for we are members of one another'. Lying is ugly in and of itself, but Paul points to something that makes it even more ugly. The thought of deceit within the Christian fellowship makes lying even more repulsive. Paul is going beyond the Mosaic law. 'You shall not bear false testimony' was one of the ten commandments – but Paul goes higher than the Mosaic law in what he says. We belong to each other! It is terrible to be trying to deceive fellow-members in the body of the Lord Jesus Christ.

It is notable that Paul obviously has Christians in mind. 'His neighbour' in this passage clearly means our fellow Christian. Why does he specially ask us to tell the truth to Christians? Are we not to tell the truth to others as well? Yes, we are, but Paul's concern is with the Christian fellowship. The church of Jesus Christ ought to be a loving fellowship which is a testimony to the world.

2. **Anger**. There are times when we ought to be angry. *'Be angry but do not sin. Let not the sun go down on your anger* (4:26), *and do not give opportunity to the devil'* (4:27). The **absence** of anger is often a sign of complacency. Think how Jesus was angry at the hardness of heart which characterised the Jewish leaders of His day. Think how He made a whip and drove out money-changers from the temple. He did not regard anger as always sinful.

Yet most of the time when we get angry we are getting angry about the wrong thing and in the wrong way. It is being bad tempered and easily angered that Paul condemns. 'Do not let the sun go down on your anger' says Paul. He means 'Settle the issue and recover your calmness before the day is ended'. It is to be noted, he does not say 'Let not the sun rise on your anger'. Is this important? I think it is. Oftentimes when we are angry we are tempted to go to bed angry, but the next day we take no notice of what happened. The sun does not **rise** on our anger. But Paul asks for something better and greater than this. It is no good pretending the next day that nothing happened, and expecting things to disappear just because you act as if nothing happened. This is 'Not letting the sun **rise** on your anger'. Paul says: deal with matter **before** the day is ended. Recover peace and harmony **before** the day ends.

Anger gives opportunity to the devil. Some disastrous mistakes and temptations and sins come if anger continues unquenched.

3. **Stealing**. Paul's third detail concerns theft. *'Let the thief no longer steal, but rather let him do some hard work, doing something honest with his own hands, so that he may have*

something to give to those in need' (4:28). Again we notice how far above the Mosaic law this command is. Paul is **not** simply repeating the Mosaic law. The law said 'Six days you shall labour' and 'You shall not steal'. The Christian gospel **fulfils** the law but it is not 100% identical to it. There is no legislation about six days as there was in the Mosaic law. And the gospel adds details about generosity to others that was never mentioned in the Ten Commandments. Life in the Spirit fulfils and goes beyond life under the Mosaic law.

4. **Talk**. *'Let no corrupt talk come out of your mouth, but only what is good for meeting the need of the occasion. Your purpose should be to minister grace to those who hear you* (4:29). *And do not grieve the Holy Spirit of God, in whom you were sealed for the day of redemption* (4:30). The Greek of verse 29 more literally says 'Every corrupt word – let it not proceed out of your mouth'. It gives the impression that something corrupt and ugly is 'on the tip of your tongue', but Paul says 'Let it not come out!'

Paul asks for godly and sweet talk. The Christian is to hate indelicate, coarse, foolish talk as an ugly thing, and not talk in the way the world talks. How much of worldly conversation is slanderous, sceptical, cynical, bitter. What precious things sinners make jokes about. How self-centred and self-admiring it all is.

Christian talk should – says Paul – have these three characteristics. (i) It must be good and suitable for the occasion. (ii) It should be helpful and minister God's grace to those who listen to us. (iii) It should not grieve the Holy Spirit. The sealing of the Spirit gives us great assurance and joy, but something of that joy will be lost if we grieve the Spirit by the way we talk.

Chapter 23

Kindness

(Ephesians 4:31–5:2)

We have seen four of Paul's detailed concerns. 1. Telling the truth. 2. Anger. 3. Stealing. 4. Talk. There are two more. He goes on to deal with kindness (4:31–5:2), and then a group that we can call the common sins of the world (5:3–7).

5. **Kindness** (Ephesians 4:31–5:2). Paul is still dealing with some of the details in his appeal for Christian godliness. He continues: *'Let all bitterness and wrath and anger and shouting and slander be put away from you with all malice* (4:31). *And become kind to one another, compassionate, forgiving each other, as God in Christ forgave you'* (4:32).

As so often he puts the matter negatively (4:31) and then positively (4:32a), and then follows up what he has said with arguments and reasons (4:32b–5:2).

First comes the negative (4:31). The Christian is to put away bitterness (getting a sour spirit because of grievances and grudges) and wrath and anger and shouting and slander. They must be got rid of; so must every kind of malice. These words are only too easy to understand! Paul uses more than one word for anger because there are different kinds of anger and people show anger in different ways. Some are violent in their manner; other are deeply resentful. Shouting is noisy; slander can be quiet.

We notice Paul does not tell us to pray about these things. Nor does he tell us we need a deliverance ministry to have them cast out of our lives. Nor does he think we need counselling. He just tells us to take action. Do it! – he says to us. Let these things be put away.

Then he becomes more positive. 'And be kind to one another, compassionate, forgiving each other...'. Again, the words are not difficult to understand. We must positively get into the habit of daily persistent kindness. The fruit of the Spirit is ... kindness. If we are being led by the Spirit we are being led into kindness. We are to become compassionate, tender-hearted people.

We are to become forgiving people. All the great saints of God have had to learn this. Joseph had to forgive his brothers. David had to forgive Saul. The prophets had to forgive their persecutors. Job had to forgive his three friends. Jesus had to forgive Judas. It means we freely forget what people have done to us, and how they have hurt us.

He reminds us of God's kindness towards us. When God asks us to be kind to others He is only asking us to treat others in the way in which He has dealt with us. You are to be 'forgiving ... as God in Christ forgave you'. Christ has come to us and said 'Your sins are forgiven'. He forgave us all our sins. After Jesus has shown us such love, how can we now hold on to our animosities towards others? It does not matter how terribly they sinned against us. We have to forgive.

Ephesians 5:1–2 develop the point further. *'And become, therefore, imitators of God as beloved children (5:1). And walk in love as Christ loved us and gave Himself up for us, a sweet-smelling offering and sacrifice to God'* (5:2).

God made us His beloved children. We are to become imitators of God as beloved children (5:1). We mimic Him, copy Him, by the joy we have in our great salvation. We do to others what He had done for us. A child learns to be like his parents. To be a 'child' of God is to represent God in this world by being like Him. The new person is created to be like God in true righteousness (4:24).

Christ has loved us, so we walk in love in a way that corresponds to what Christ has done for us. This means that the more we feel Christ's love, the easier it is to love other people. We were so undeserving. There was nothing that was worthy of the love of Jesus. Maybe you see nothing deserving in the other person. Why should I love him? Why should I love her? He does not deserve my love. But you did not deserve Jesus' love! Love is not only for those who deserve it! There is nothing specially wonderful about loving those who are nice to you. Jesus did not die for His friends. He died for His enemies. He died 'for' us. He did for us what we could not do for ourselves. This is the love of God, the kind of love that God wants us to show to everyone everywhere.

Christ's love was practical and sacrificial. He gave Himself up for us. Love is largely a matter of giving, yielding, surrendering. What self-surrender was involved when Jesus set His face to go to the cross. He was a real man and so shrunk from suffering, as we all do. 'If it be possible, take this cup from me', He prayed. If there was any other way that He could go to save the human race, He would have preferred to go another way. But there was no other way. The human race could not be saved without the cross. It was the Father's will for His Son. The way of love for men and women involved terrible self-surrender. But Jesus was willing to do it! He said 'I shall give way to what I know has to be done. Not My will but Your will be done'. Love is doing what has to be done for others, no matter what it costs us.

Christ's sacrifice pleased God. It was a sweet-smelling offering and sacrifice to God (5:2). Christ's sacrifice pleased God, and when we sacrifice ourselves so as to be kind to others we too shall be giving a sweet-smelling offering and sacrifice to God.

Chapter 24

Inheritance in the Kingdom

(Ephesians 5:3–7)

Paul is dealing with some details of the call to godliness: truth (4:25), anger (4:26–27), stealing (4:28), talk (4:29–30), kindness (4:31–5:2). Now (4:25–5:7) he brings in a string of topics that were the common sins of the ancient world – as they are of our world too!

6. **The common sins of the ancient world** (5:3–7). *'And immorality and every kind of uncleanness or covetousness – let them not even be named among you, as befits holy people* (5:3). *And let there be no filthiness and foolish talk or levity, which are not fitting, but rather let there be thanksgiving'* (5:4). Paul does not give detailed attention to these things to the extent that he has had things to say about truth, anger, stealing, talking, kindness. It is as if these matters are so loathsome to him, he mentions them only to say let them not even be named!

Again his style of arguing is distinctively Christian. He does not warn about the health hazards of immorality or the damage that covetousness does to the national economy. His style of arguing is utterly different from the typical philosopher or teacher of ethics. It is not the church's job to teach common morality in the same way that a host of religions and ideologies do. The Christian way is unique and distinctive. Its method is to appeal to us in term of our being the people of God. He reminds us of who we are and what we believe. We turn aside from these sins 'as befits holy people', or because 'they are not fitting' for people for whom God has done so much. The appeal is to what has happened to us in the Lord Jesus Christ.

So he urges us to keep well away from every kind of immorality. We should not even want to think about such sins or discuss them. They are to be rejected with horror. He includes covetousness alongside sins of immorality. There are people who would never be tempted into immorality, but they are guilty of covetousness which is just as bad. And in the same breath he includes foolish talk or levity – a style of talking which is coarse, frivolous, careless. His words do not exclude humour – Jesus could be humorous at times – but they exclude the type of humour which is hurtful, self-centred, slapdash. Paul asks that our talk should instead be full of the kind of happiness and contentment that leads to thanksgiving.

Paul closes off this little unit with two warnings, one about the present time, another about the future. First, there is a **warning about the present**. *'For you must know this: no person who is immoral or unclean or covetousness – and such a person is an idolater – has any inheritance in the kingdom of God and of Christ'* (5:5). I do not think Paul is questioning any one's salvation. He knows that the true Christian might fall into sins such as these (otherwise why raise the matter at all?) Nor is Paul thinking of the future judgement (which is more in mind in the next verse). His tenses are present tenses, 'No person who is **at this present time** immoral or unclean or covetousness – and is **at this present time** an idolater – has **at this present time** any inheritance in the kingdom of God and of Christ (5:5). Obviously such a person might have been wicked in the past and yet be enjoying God's kingdom (for forgiveness and new life is open to the wicked). Nor is he denying that Christians can fall into such sins (obviously they can). Nor is he saying that forgiveness and restoration is impossible for a 'backslider'. And he knows that there is such a thing as being 'saved through fire' (1 Corinthians 3:15).

The point of verse 5 is that **at this time** such sins are a blockage to the enjoyment of the kingdom. There is no way a person can be indulging in sins of this nature and yet be experiencing the blessings of the kingdom of God. We cannot 'dwell in God's holy hill' (Psalm 15:1) and be sinning at the same time. 'Inheritance' has to do with reward, present or future. Here the point deals with the present. Those who do not 'sow to the Spirit' (Galatians 6:8) do not reap from the Spirit. Instead they are reaping ruination for themselves.

Verse 7 moves to a warning about the future. *'Let no one deceive you with empty words, for on account of these things the wrath of God is coming upon the children of disobedience* (5:6). *Do not become partakers with them'* (5:7).

A day of judgement is on its way. God's anger will be poured out on sin and sinners. The sins Paul has just mentioned will be purified out of God's world. The fires of God's anger will consume sin. Only he who does the will of God will abide for ever. Elsewhere Paul assures the Christian that he will be saved from God's wrath when it comes (1 Thessalonians 1:10; Romans 5:10). There is no condemnation for the Christian (Romans 8:1).

Yet here he has a different angle on the matter. The wrath of God only comes upon the 'children of disobedience' and the Christian is not a 'child of disobedience'. Yet at the same time it must be said that if (contrary to his new birth and his position in God's kingdom) he is a 'partaker' with the wicked in their sins, then such a person can expect to be a 'partaker' in the wrath of God in judgement. The wrath of God is coming upon the children of disobedience, but the Christian might be **'hurt** by the second death' (Revelation 2:11) and suffer loss at the judgement seat of Christ (1 Corinthians 3:15) and lose 'reward' in a fiery judgement (Hebrews 10:26–31; note 'reward' in 10:35). The **righteous** who have had a share in the sins of the disobedient will experience the anger of God. There is no point in saying to Christians 'Because of these things the wrath of God is coming' if that wrath cannot touch them at all. 1 Corinthians 3:15 makes it clear that the anger of God against the sins of His people does not mean the undoing of their justification or the cancelling of their sonship or the removal of their new birth. It is justification, adoption and new birth which are eternally secure. However the hope of receiving 'inheritance' or the possibility of experiencing God's anger by forfeiting reward, are still open-ended possibilities.

Chapter 25

Walking in the Light

(Ephesians 5:7–12)

Verse 7 winds up the small unit in 4:25–5:6, but it also prepares the way for a new angle of approach in 5:8–17. *'Do not become partakers with them,'* says Paul (5:7). Then he gives a reason which opens up a new way of putting his appeal for godly living. *'For you were once darkness, but now you are light in the Lord. Walk as children of the light* (5:8). *For the fruit of the light consists of all goodness and right-eousness and truth* (5:9). *Find out what is the will of the Lord* (5:10). *And do not be joined together with the fruitless works of darkness, but rather expose them* (5:11). *For it is shameful even to mention the things which are done by them in secret'* (5:12).

1. First of all Paul appeals to us to remember who we are and what has happened to us (5:8–9). **Christian godliness is a matter of putting into effect what has happened to them**. Paul asks the Christians at Ephesus and any other Christians who read his letter to realise what has happened to them. A radical and momentous change has taken place in their lives. We must notice that Paul does not say 'Once you were **in** the darkness, but now you are **in** the light . . .'. It is not a change of the realms in which they live that he speaks of (although he could have done that as well). It is a change in the Ephesian Christians **themselves** that he refers to. They themselves were darkness. They themselves have changed and are no longer what they used to be. The Lord Jesus Christ is the 'light of the world', but they are so transformed so as to belong to Jesus Christ, and the result is that they

also are the light of the world. Not only are they in the light; the light is in them, and they have been transformed.

So what follows is perfectly logical. *'Walk as children of the light'* (5:8). This is the New Testament way of calling for godliness. We are asked to be what we are! The New Testament tells us certain things about who we are and what has happened to us. Then it says to us, 'Now then, if this is what has happened to you . . .'. The New Testament spends a lot of time explaining to us in great detail how a great change has come into our lives and it insists that we are not the people we used to be. Paul does not call un-Christian people to live the Christian life. He is speaking here to people who have experienced what it is to come to faith in Christ and become new people altogether. The secret of godly living is to take notice of this word that God gives us, telling us about ourselves. The truth sets us free.

Darkness spoke of sin and shame and spiritual blindness. Before we came to faith in Jesus we were darkness. It was our very nature to be spiritually blind. We enjoyed being far from God. We loved the darkness that was in us. But then a very great change took place. Now we are light 'in the Lord'. It is the Lord Jesus Christ who makes the difference. We are what we are because we are 'in' Him; we are joined on to Him. His life is within us. We now have to be logical! We put into action what we actually are.

Paul tells us what it means in practice. *'For the fruit of the light consists of all goodness and righteousness and truth'* (5:9). It is a general description of the 'fruit of the light', a description of what this new nature in us will actually lead to. It will result in **goodness**: kindness, benevolence, sweetness towards other people. Our new nature will result in **righteousness**: integrity. uprightness, straight dealings with other people. Our new nature will result in **truth**: openness, the opposite of hiddenness, darkness and shame.

2. Next, having asked us to remember who we are and what has happened to us (5:8–9), **he goes on to give us fuller details** (5:10–14).

One detail concerning **knowing God's will**. *'Find out what is the will of the Lord'* (5:10). The Christian is to discover what really pleases God, what God likes. It is the Lord Jesus Christ Himself who is His first concern. The Christian is relating to a person, the Lord Jesus Christ! He seeks to live a life of goodness, righteousness, truth, because He want to find out Jesus' will in every situation.

Another detail concerns **our being distinctive people** who do not become so similar to the ungodly that our position is inconsistent. *'And do not be joined together with the fruitless works of darkness, but rather expose them'* (5:11). The ungodly do 'works'; the godly produce 'fruit'. The two different words reveal the difference between the pagan and the Christian. The unsaved person does 'works'; the word emphasises that what comes out in the life of the ungodly is something he or she does purely from himself. But what comes from the Christian is the 'fruit' of the new thing that God has put in him. The Christian does not share the sinful interests of the ungodly. Instead we get them to see something entirely different. We walk in purity and it makes the sinner feel the shame of what he or she is doing.

We ourselves are to have **a true sense of shame**. *'For it is shameful even to mention the things which are done by them in secret'* (5:12). It is a terrible thing when we get so used to sin that we no longer are able to be ashamed. The Christian is sensitive. Certain things fill him with shame. He does not even like to mention them. We do not rebuke others merely by being negative. We demonstrate the joy of the Lord, and the world can see that we have something they do not have.

Chapter 26

Using the Time Wisely
(Ephesians 5:13–17)

Verse 13 is still continuing this theme of being a light to the world. 'The light' is the light of the Lord Jesus Christ. The Christian is 'in the Lord'; so like Jesus he or she is a light in the world. The Christian, when he is rejoicing in the Lord and living as he should, exposes the world. *'And all things become visible when exposed to the light...'* says Paul, *'for everything that is illuminated becomes light.'* The first part of the sentence means that the Christian's light makes visible the spiritual situation around him. Sin is seen as sin. Righteousness is seen as righteousness. Christ is seen as the Saviour. The Christian makes everything visible. 'All things become visible when exposed to the light'. 'I am the light of the world' said Jesus. 'He that follows me shall not walk in darkness'. Christians are lights in the world when they follow Jesus. Light shines out of them in what they do and what they say. It has the effect of revealing the world to be what it is: dark, sinful, gloomy, boring, dreary in its endless quest for pleasures, rebellious against God, hateful towards others. When the Christian is what he ought to be, it is like flashing a bright beam into the darkness. The point of the next clause (*'for everything that is illuminated becomes light'*) is that light turns the thing it shines on into light also. Brightness makes other things bright. The Christian's light brings the dark world into the light also; we see it as it is. The darkness of the world becomes light in the sense that it no longer remains hidden once the light of the Christian draws near.

If we are following Paul's trend of thought, verse 14 will be a summary of the Christian's message to the world.

'For this reason, it says,
wake, sleeper,
and arise from the dead,
and Christ will shine on you' (5:14).

A piece of poetry is quoted. It is probably three lines of a Christian hymn. The Christian knows the world is deep in the sleep of spiritual death. Yet the Christian calls to the world in what he says and how he lives. 'Wake up!', say the Christians to the world. 'You are in the sleep of spiritual death. You are in danger. Believe in Jesus. Arise from your spiritual death. And Christ will shine on you'.

Verse 15 moves on. If verses 8–14 were a call to walk as children of light, then verses 15–17 call them to walk as children of wisdom. Verse 15 puts the basic appeal. *'Therefore be careful how you walk, not as unwise people but as wise people . . . '* (5:15). Then verses 16 and 17 spell out what is involved: *'. . . as wise people* (5:15), *making the most of the time for the days are evil* (5:16). *So then, do not become foolish but understanding what is the will of the Lord'* (5:17).

The Christian is 'light in the Lord', so he or she has the ability to be wise. Wisdom is skill at living. It is not the same as knowledge. One can have a lot of knowledge and yet be a fool. There are plenty of people who know a lot yet are not skilful in the way they live. The Christian also knows a lot but – more important – is able to be skilful in the way in which he lives. **Foolishness** is being governed by desires and impulses, hates and loves. It is short-term impulsiveness. **Wisdom** is the exact opposite. It thinks. It takes time. It gets down to consider the situation. It considers consequences. It takes a long view. It considers the end from the beginning. It looks at the whole as well as the parts. It takes everything into consideration; it has a kind of all-roundedness, and looks at things from every side. Be careful how you walk, says Paul. It means that we take time considering what we are doing. We spend time with the Lord seeking His blessing and His presence. Then we weigh our actions and our attitudes in the presence of the Lord.

We are to *'make the most of the time for the days are evil'* (5:16). We should use our time wisely. Most Christians need a kind of 'structure' to their lives. It does not have to be rigid or legalistic. It should take into account our physical nature (some people can hardly get moving in the mornings; others are bursting with energy at the crack of dawn). Our hobbies should be ones that are truly helpful to us. Recreations should re-create! We do not throw away the day on foolish trivial things. For myself as a pastor–preacher I have a simple structure, which fits the way I'm made, and fits the way we do things in the Kenyan churches. The structure of most people will be different from mine! You find your own!

The secret of 'making the most of the time' is (i) keeping to a basic structure. In many kinds of work it is structured for you! I don't easily let anything interrupt my mornings, when I want to be praying, meditating, writing. (ii) Making sure you block out chunks of your time for work, for meditation and prayer, for family and friends, for relaxation, and for the calling God has laid upon your life. (iii) Grabbing opportunities to speak for the Lord Jesus Christ.

Then I have a different lay-out of my time for when I am travelling, and another one for when I take a more restful day or am on a short holiday. It does not have to be legalistic. There is room for sudden changes. I can still follow the leading of the Holy Spirit. But we have to 'make the most of the time'. The days in which we live are evil – all of them until the second coming of Jesus! I don't mind how **you** do it. Do it your own way, but make the most of the time! The days are evil.

'So then, do not become foolish but understanding what is the will of the Lord' (5:17). In the way you spend your time,

stay in touch with the Lord. Know His will. Pray without ceasing. And – I assume you have come to salvation in Christ – your life will be a fruitful one I promise.

Chapter 27

Becoming Full of the Holy Spirit
(Ephesians 5:18–21)

Paul now has yet another way of urging us to live godly lives. *'And do not get drunk with wine, in which is dissipation, but be filled by the Spirit* (5:18), *communicating to one another with psalms and hymns and spiritual songs, singing and making melody with your heart to the Lord* (5:19), *giving thanks always for all things in the name of the Lord Jesus Christ to God-and-Father* (5:20), *being subject to one another in the fear of Christ'* (5:21).

Paul's theme here is the godly life. That has been his theme all along. Since 4:17 every verse has been exhorting us to godly living or supporting an appeal for godly living. The theme is the same here. It has three parts to it: an ungodliness we must avoid ('Do not get drunk ...'); a fullness that we must show ('but be filled by the Spirit') and some results or accompaniments which attend the fullness of the Spirit.

1. **An ungodliness we must avoid**. 'Do not get drunk with wine', he says. That was the way they got their stimulus and excitement in the old days before their conversion. But that kind of stimulus squanders one's resources and is eventually destructive. In that kind of life there is 'dissipation' – exhaustion, wasting one's money, damaging one's health. Excess alcohol is depressing not stimulating!

2. **A fullness that must characterise our lives**. 'Be filled by the Spirit' says Paul. There is a kind of similarity between the fullness of the Spirit and taking excess alcohol – although they are very different also. The similarity is this. The

worldly man uses beer and wine to get himself to feel good, to give himself a mood of relaxation, to make him convivial. Wine makes him talk freely; he may even start singing! But Paul knows there is a better way. The Holy Spirit leads us to feel good. He also gives us a mood of relaxed confidence and authority. The Holy Spirit makes us convivial. By the Spirit we talk of Jesus freely and boldly. In the Holy Spirit we like to sing! There is a similarity between the two kinds of fullness, but one is destructive and the other is wonderful and liberating.

What does 'Be filled by the Spirit' mean? A study of the words 'fill', 'filled' and 'fullness' will show that these words are used in a very varied way to speak of at least two different ideas. (i) It can be used of a sudden blessing or something that happens of one specific occasion. People can **suddenly** enabled to sing a song (see Luke 1:41) or to speak with tongues (see Acts 2:4) or to reply powerfully to an enemy (see Acts 4:8) or to speak boldly on one special occasion (see Acts 4:31). I could call this a **special** filling. (ii) But then the word is used in another way, it can refer to a **constant** characteristic of one's life. Godly and spiritually powerful men and women are said to be 'full' of the Spirit. Barnabas was 'full of the Holy Spirit' (Acts 11:24). The people chosen as deacons had to be 'full of the Spirit' as the regular characteristic of their lives (Acts 6:3). There are yet other ways in which the words are used (sometimes speaking of more than one thing happening at the same time). The question is: how is the word being used here in Ephesians 5:18? It is certainly in the second way. Paul is calling us to be regularly and constantly obedient to and rejoicing in the Holy Spirit. There are three reasons for saying that the word 'filled' refers to the second of these ideas, not the first. (i) The **context** from 4:17–6:20 all the way through is dealing with godly living. Ephesians 5:18–21 is simply coming at the same subject from a slightly new angle. (ii) The **tense** is a present tense. It does not refer to something sudden or dramatic. It refers to something constantly and steady. (iii) Nowhere in the New Testament is a person **commanded** to be filled with the Spirit in the 'sudden' sense of the term. But we are **commanded** to work out our salvation and be 'full' of the Holy Spirit in the second sense. It means that we submit ourselves to the Holy Spirit. We listen to Him. We obey Him. We are 'full' of Him in the sense that He rules us and He finds no blockages or hindrances in us.

3. **Some signs and accompaniments of this yielding to the Spirit**. What exactly is the relationship between the basic command here ('be filled by the Spirit') and the five phrases that follow ('communicating ... singing ... making melody ... giving thanks ... being subject ... ')? 'Communicating to one another' should not be translated 'Speaking'. You do not 'speak' a psalm or hymn!

These are different **aspects** of being full of the Spirit. A person who yields himself to God the Holy Spirit will be someone who has fellowship with others, a person who sings, a person who is thankful to God, and a person who gets along well with other Christians. The words here are plural. Paul is referring to something that we all do together. Growing in holiness is not something isolated or lonely. Christians learn together to be full of the Spirit and express their joy to God in song and thankfulness.

Yielding to the Holy Spirit will show itself in our submissiveness to each other. It means we keep in mind that we are part of a fellowship. We cease to be self-assertive and self-centred and we each put the whole 'body of Christ' before ourselves. We do so 'in the fear of Christ', that is, eager to avoid missing Christ's rewards, eager to avoid Christ's chastening. Obedience is not something cold or isolated. We are living the godly life when the Spirit is working unhindered in us all and we are 'communicating ... singing ... making melody ... giving thanks ... being subject' to the needs of the people of God around us.

Chapter 28

Wives and Husbands

(Ephesians 5:22–26)

Paul now moves on to deal with relationships. He has given a general appeal (4:17–24) and has considered some detailed matters (4:25–5:7). He has put the appeal for godliness in some other ways (5:8–21). Now he comes to deal with relationships. Christian godliness involves relating skilfully to people who are close to us: husbands, wives, children, parents, workers, employees.

Wives are to model themselves on the submissiveness of the church. Paul begins: *'Wives, subject yourselves to your own husbands, as something you do for the Lord'* (5:22). The Greek word 'subject yourselves' is not actually present in verse 22. It carries over from verse 21. More literally it reads: 'Submit to one another ... Wives to husbands...'. Sometimes too much is made of this, as if wifely submission was **only part** of mutual submission, and Paul really means that husbands must also submit to wives as well (which he does not say!). It is true that there is such a thing as **mutual** submission among all Christians across all relationships (5:21), but this does not cancel out what is dealt with in 5:22–33, and the fact that the verb is carried over from verse 21 does not change this. Paul does not call husbands to be submissive to wives, or parents to obey children, or masters to obey slaves! Verse 21 does not cancel out the leadership patterns of 5:22 through to 6:9. And the verb is present in verse 24!

'Wives, subject yourselves to your own husbands, as some-

thing you do for the Lord' (5:22). It does **not** mean that the wife is in any way inferior. She is not less human, or less Christian. It does **not** mean that she is less gifted, less intelligent – or anything along those lines! It means that in the team-work between husband and wife, the husband is the team-leader.

'For the husband is the head of the wife as also Christ is the head of the church, and is himself the Saviour of the body (5:23). *As the church submits to Christ . . . '* The Greek begins 'But as the church submits . . . ', yet it is not likely that it is a contrast with anything in verse 23. The Greek *alla* seems to means 'But to go back to what I was saying about husbands . . . '. I leave it untranslated. *'As the church submits to Christ so should wives submit to their husbands in everything'* (5:24). 'Head' means 'ruler', 'leader'. Sometimes an attempt is made to avoid the thrust of Paul's teaching by understanding the word translated 'head' as 'source'. But certainly in this passage the meaning 'source' does not fit. The husband is the team-leader of a marriage, as Christ is the leader of His church. The wife is to follow a husband's lead; it does not mean she is without a voice or is timid. It simply means that the **final** decisions in the home are the husband's responsibility. He does not have the only word, but he has the last word. Why should there be any difficulty over this? Anglicans have bishops who can be quite autocratic, sports teams have captains, industries have managers, charismatic churches have 'lead-elders' – and marriages have husbands! Why should one form of leadership be thought wrong, but in every other department of life moderate hierarchy and leadership are seen to be necessary? Absolute equality of leadership-position is practised nowhere else. Why should the Christian view of marriage be an exception to what is recognised everywhere? Teams need leaders, even a team of two.

Christ is the head of the church and 'Saviour of the body'. Ephesians 5:23 picks up from 1:22. This last phrase is a strong hint to the husband that he would help his wife's submission if he too, like Jesus, were a protector and rescuer of his wife when the situation calls for it.

Jesus has plans for His church. The church finds out His will and follows His lead. So – says the New Testament – *'should wives submit to their husbands in everything'*. Everything! It is quite an extreme statement! Paul will have some extreme statements for men too in Ephesians 5:25–33. There are limits, however. A wife does not have to follow the lead of the husband if he wants her to sin. The principle of Acts 5:29 applies.

Does this instruction apply even if the husband is not a Christian? 1 Peter 3:1–6 lets us know that the answer is 'yes'. The wife is not to act one-sidedly in anything. She consults her husband on all major decisions. A Christian husband should not stifle his wife (of course not!) or act insensitively. On the other hand the wife does not submit to her husband only on **condition** that he is as sensitive as she would like him to be. He may not even be a Christian at all. She follows her husband's lead (generally speaking) as something she does for the Lord Jesus Christ, not as something she does for her husband because he is such a deserving person!

Paul addresses the wife first. He wants **first** the basic structure required by God to be accepted. He addresses the one **under** authority before he addresses the one **in** authority. Then he is able to turn to the one **in** authority and tell him to make use of his responsibility with a loving attitude.

Husbands model themselves on the love of Jesus. Paul moves from wives to husbands. He puts forward the Lord Jesus Christ as a model for the husband. *'Husbands, love your wives, as Christ also loved the church and gave Himself for her* (5:25), *in order that He might sanctify her, cleansing her by the washing of the water through the word'* (5:26). As soon as Paul talks about a husband's love he switches to talk about Jesus' love for the church. Upon the cross Jesus gave Himself up as a sacrifice, in great love (5:25). Christ is the husband of the church. He came to this world as a bride-groom seeking a bride. His purpose on the cross was that He might do what needed to be done for sinners to be cleansed and become His bride. In spite of all the sin and wickedness which He saw in sinners, He showed great love. He did not reject His church because of her weaknesses and sins. He took the practical step of sacrificing Himself for her upon the cross. His purpose on the cross was to 'sanctify' the church, to put the church once-and-for-ever into the position of being special to God, and then continue the process of cleansing in her life. The thought is similar to Titus 2:14. The prospective bride of Ezekiel 16 received a cleansing bath and a new set of clothes and then is presented to the prospective husband. Christ humbled Himself in loving sacrifice upon the cross. His purpose was that He might 'sanctify the church, cleansing her'. The cleansing is the means by which the sanctifying takes place.

Chapter 29

Christ and His Church
(Ephesians 5:26–33)

It is generally thought that 'the washing of the water with the word' in Ephesians 5:26 refers to water-baptism, but (i) Ezekiel 16 surely does not refer to water-baptism, and the imagery is taken from there. (ii) This is a washing of the **whole** church; Paul does not usually think of water-baptism as a washing in which Christ washes the whole church in a single ceremony using water. (iii) It is difficult to see exactly how in practical terms baptismal-water sanctifies the church. Is it that my getting baptised when I first believed in Jesus is now having a sanctifying effect on me? Certainly my **faith** still plays a part, but does the water? Or did some sprinkling of water on a child actually show itself in a sanctified life? It must be 'invisible grace'! Is water-baptism a ceremony which sanctifies the whole church in one act – all water-baptisms being viewed as one? An interpretation which cannot be translated into practical terms for the Christian – without extreme superstition – is by that very fact unlikely. The Christian lives by realities, not impractical theories!

To say the water-baptism 'represents' something is true in itself, but it is not the language used here. Here in Ephesians 5 the use of the term 'water' is imagery and metaphor – picture language. Christ died on the cross in order to make it possible for Him to consecrate the church to Himself and – as a process throughout the history of the church – 'wash' the church from her sinful ways. The phrase 'through the word' explains what the metaphor means and what the 'washing' consists of. As elsewhere in Scripture, God 'washes' us by the use of His word – the entire gospel message (see John 17:17). The truth makes us free (see John 8:31–32).

There was a further purpose in Christ's love for the church. Christ loved the church and gave Himself ... cleansing her ... *'in order that He might present the church to Himself as a glorious church, without spot or wrinkle or anything of that nature but that she might be holy and blameless'* (5:27). Paul is speaking of Christ's future plans for His bride. He intends to bring her to a high level of purity. The gates of hell will not defeat Christ's church. She will succeed in being ready for Jesus' coming. In Ezekiel 16:10–14 the Lord's bride is beautiful. Jesus' church will have reached a high level of maturity before Jesus comes. Paul uses all this as a model for the husband; the husband is to be concerned about his wife's future.

A husband's love for his wife is like love of his own flesh. Paul goes on. *'In the same way husbands also should love their wives as their own bodies. He who loves his own wife loves himself* (5:28), *for no one ever hated his own flesh, but he nourishes it and cherishes it as Christ does the church* (5:29), *for we are members of his body'* (5:30). (The words 'of his flesh and of his bones' – compare the King James version of 1611 – are found in some manuscripts but were added by scribes; they are not original.) A man likes to look after himself. He protects himself, he feeds himself. He takes care of himself. Paul says, 'Your wife is part of you. You have become one flesh. You cannot damage her without damaging yourself.' Christ feels the same way about His church. He protects and cares for His church from the heavenly throne.

A husband's love for his wife is above that of his wider family. *'"For this reason a man shall leave his father and his mother and be joined to his wife, and the two shall become one flesh"* (5:31). *This mystery is great, but I am speaking about Christ and about the church'* (5:32). The husband must not live in the old way once he is married. He 'leaves his father and his mother'. His old priorities no longer apply. He puts his wife above anything that was in his old life.

Paul gives us a hint that these topics need careful meditation – much greater than can be given here. Marriage is a profound mystery. Let everyone ponder it long and hard. He or she will learn great lessons of wisdom and sanctification. It is the hardest and toughest environment in which to work out godliness! It brings the greatest joys and if it goes wrong it brings the greatest sufferings. It is easy to be nice to people you don't see so often; marriage is a tougher testing ground.

The theme of marriage is also the most illuminating way of understanding the gospel. It is not surprising that there is a whole book of the Bible about romance and marriage (the Song of Songs). It is the greatest parable ever of the Christian life. 'This mystery is great, but I am speaking about Christ and about the church' (5:32). If you begin to see into the mystery, you begin to see what it means for Christ to have love us and for Him to go on loving us. You begin to see how precious the church is to Jesus.

Paul closes with a two-point summary. *'To summarise: let each one of you also so love his wife as he loves himself, and let the wife respect her husband'* (5:33). It might seem surprising that he has only two things to say: love and submission, one point for the husbands, one for the wives. Why does he not have a fuller number of pieces of advice? Why does he not tell wives to love their husbands? His two points are the key to all other matters. If the wife is a woman who allows her husband to be the leader and 'chairman', if husband is a man of love, all be well. There may be a thousand things to be attended to, but they have a starting point. But if either of these matters is disobeyed, they have no starting-point for recovery.

Chapter 30

Relationships in the Lord
(Ephesians 6:1–9)

Paul continues to deal with different kinds of relationship. It is still the theme of Ephesians 5:18. The Holy Spirit will help is in having good relationships. The 'fullness of the Spirit' works itself out eventually in attitudes to husbands and wives, parents and children, employers and employees. These subjects are too vast to be dealt with in a few lines, but Paul gives us a few starting-points.

1. **He has a word for Christian children**. Paul's instruction in 5:22–6:9 shows that he is concerned about Christian families. Paul had no family himself. If he was ever married, he was not married during the years of his ministry. Perhaps he was never married. Perhaps he was a widower. Perhaps his wife left him when he came to faith in Christ. One might feel that he was not qualified to speak on such matters. But the word of God is the word of God whether we feel qualified or not. In any case, who can feel himself to be an expert in such matters as these? Is there a perfect husband? A perfect wife? A perfect parent? Paul says, *'Children obey your parents, as something you do in union with the Lord; for this is right'* (6:1). Christian children must give honour, respect, obedience to their parents. As always there are limits. Acts 5:19 applies here as well. God created people to be in families. He expects the family structures to be taken notice of. People will suffer if they do not do so for this is how men and women were created. Honouring

113

parents is right! *'Honour your father and mother. This is a supreme commandment with a promise:* (6:2), *that it may be well with you, and you live long on the earth'* (6:3). This verse is the only place where Paul explicitly quotes the Mosaic law in connection with Christian obedience. One must remember (i) he is following up his call to be full of the Spirit (Ephesians 5:18). Life in the Holy Spirit fulfils the law. (ii) He is expecting us to look for the Christian equivalent of the law. The fifth commandment promised national stability and continuance in the territory of Israel if the Mosaic law were kept. There is an **equivalent** for this in the life of the Christian who obeys his parents. As always the law **foreshadows** the gospel. The **exact** promise of the law does not apply (he does not have to live in Israel!) but there is a parallel. Obeying parents will lead to stability and joy in our life on planet earth.

People have been puzzled that the fifth command is said to be 'the first commandment with a promise'. Is there not a promise attached to some earlier commandments? I suggest it should be translated 'a supreme commandment' and it means that it is one of the Ten Commandments, all of which are more serious than other commands. (We recall the discussions in the gospels about greater and lesser commands.) It is 'a supreme commandment' and it has a special promise of stability attached to it. It is fulfilled in a different way from its application in the days of the Mosaic covenant (for example, there is no death penalty for disobedience as there was then). But it is to be fulfilled by those who walk in the Spirit.

2. **Paul has a word for Christian parents**. *'And parents, do not make your children angry, but bring them up in the training and admonition of the Lord'* (6:4). If children are to be obedient, parents are to give them some help also, in three ways: (i) not being unfair so as to create resentment, (ii) giving them training, (iii) giving them kindly rebuke.

3. **He has a word for Christian workers**. *'Slaves, obey your earthly masters with fear and trembling, with straight-forward*

hearts, as people obeying Christ (6:5). *And do it not to please people when they are watching you, but as servants of Christ, doing the will of God wholeheartedly* (6:6), *working with enthusiasm as to the Lord and not to other people* (6:7). *You know that each person, when he does something good, will be recompensed for this by the Lord'* (6:8). Of all 'conditions of employment', slaves in the Roman empire had what must be among the worst! If Paul can give them some good advice, then no lesser hardships of employment are impossible to live with! To slaves he gives instructions that they should be obedient, straight-forward people, fearful of displeasing God. Their motivation should be God's reward.

4. **Paul has a word for Christian employers**. *'And you masters, do the same things to them, leaving aside the use of threats, knowing that both they and you have a Master in heaven, and there is no partiality with him'* (6:9). 'Do the same' means: obey God in the way you relate to the slaves. You too remember God is watching you. You too work for their good with enthusiasm. What the slaves have to do, you also have to do.

Paul does not tell the 'Master' to release his slaves. The Christian gospel works **slowly** in these matters. It gets large numbers of people to be Christians first, before it tries to change social conditions. Slaves and masters who obeyed Ephesians 6:5–9 had drastically changed slavery within their own households and turned it into something much more friendly. Eventually Christian opinion would lead to something better, an abolition of slavery. Where there is no Christian opinion, the reverse thing happens. Free people get so ill-treated and underpaid, they gradually become slaves. There is plenty of slavery in the world still! Ephesians 6:9 is still needed.

In all of these instructions within the six-fold relationships of 5:11–6:9, the key to the matter has been expressed six times (5:22, 25; 6:1, 4, 5, 9). It is to be consciously serving the Lord Jesus Christ.

Chapter 31

Spiritual Warfare

(Ephesians 6:10–13)

Paul cannot end his letter just yet. He has been appealing for the Christians to live godly lives, yet there is a complication – the devil! He must give some attention to the subject of spiritual conflict before he closes his letter.

1. **First, we have a call to be strong**. *'Finally, be made strong in the Lord and in the might of His strength'* (6:10). Paul is about to tell us of a great conflict. This living of the Christian life has one extra difficulty, the devil. It will require strength to defeat Satan. Where can such strength come from? From the Lord Jesus Christ! Jesus has already shown Himself to be a mighty conqueror of Satan. He defeated Satan in the wilderness. Now He can give strength to us. The Christian learns to lean on Jesus. That is not everything; an armour has to be put on as well. But there is a starting-point. We have constant fellowship with the Lord Jesus Christ. We trust His promises.

2. Next comes **the call to be equipped**. *'Put on the full armour of God so that you will be able to stand against the craftiness of the devil'* (6:11). We have to be in fellowship with the Lord Jesus, and we have to trust Him to give us strength – but then we have to do certain things. 'The battle is the Lord's' but we have to fight as well. It is God's battle but He strengthens **us** to fight for Him. We have to do certain things (as we shall see) that give us victory. Paul calls it 'putting on our armour'.

3. Paul mentions **the enemy – the devil**. He is real. He is a personal being. He hates God and God's Son, our Lord Jesus Christ. He hates God's word. He hates God's people. He has great power: power over nature, power over animals, access to the heart of man. He can blind the mind. He can sow doubts. He spreads the spirit of fear and can use false teachings. He attacks us with evil thoughts, with depression, discouragement, resentment, with pride. He can hurl against us 'fiery darts' – special attacks, thorns in the flesh.

4. Next Paul mentions **the enemy's assistants**. *'For the battle that is ours is not a fight against flesh and blood, but against the principalities, against the authorities, against the world rulers of this darkness, against the spiritual forces of evil in the heavenly places'* (6:12). With Satan are a host of evil spirits who assist him. They are real. Jesus was accused of being the prince of demons (Matthew 12:22–24). He replied by speaking of a whole kingdom of spiritual beings under Satan, which is united in its hatred against God (Matthew 12:25–29). When a woman asked help for her demon-possessed daughter, He accepted what she said and eventually sent healing to her daughter (Matthew 15:22–28). He did something similar for a man with a son who was demonised (Matthew 17:14–20). On occasion He exercised His authority over a whole mass of evil spirits (Mark 5:1–16).

When we seek to live a godly life we shall find powerful opposition not only from the world and our own 'flesh' but – even more forcefully – from spiritual opposition coming from outside of us. It does not mean that we are 'possessed'. It only means that we are facing opposition. One of the secrets of the Christian life is to realise that this opposition is **not** coming from 'flesh and blood'. Our ultimate enemy is not ourselves; we have died to sin. Our ultimate enemy is not other people. Our enemy is Satan and his colleagues. There is a whole kingdom of them with different positions in that kingdom. Some are 'principalities', others 'authorities', others 'world rulers' or 'spiritual forces of evil'. Like Satan, they are personal beings, spiritual beings without bodies. They are unclean and have power to attack God's people.

5. Paul assures us of **the hope of victory**. *'So because of this you must take up the full armour of God, in order that you may be able to resist in the evil day, and having done all things to be standing'* (6:13).

This is the good news! The devil and his agents are resistible! Despite their very great power, Jesus is stronger than they. If we are 'in the Lord' and if we put on our spiritual armour we are able to withstand even their mighty strength, because the mighty strength of Jesus is greater. We are not to be surprised at this conflict or afraid. We are to stand! Our Lord Jesus is there at our side. He is ready to give us assistance. We have to fight but Jesus is near at hand. Sometimes when the battle is strong He will draw specially close and will say to us 'I am with you ... no one shall attack you to harm you...' (Acts 18:9–10). There is a great atmosphere of victory in these words. Can you hear them? 'Be made strong in the Lord! ... You will be able to stand ... you must take up the full armour of God ... to resist in the evil day, and having done all things to be standing.' There is a great sense of triumph in these words. Almighty power is at work for us and in us. The secret of victory is to know that the Lord Jesus Christ is strong and yet He is willing to impart His strength to us. We see our strength in Jesus. We look at the victories of His life, His miracles, His wisdom, His conquering Satan and all his friends. And then we recall that same 'might of His strength' is available for us. We are 'in Him'. His strength is ours. We live by the faithfulness of the Son of God.

Chapter 32

The Christian's Armour

(Ephesians 6:14–17)

Paul is dealing with his last major topic in this letter: spiritual warfare. He has told his friends that they must be strong in the Lord and they must put on an armour provided for them. Verses 14–20 now give us fuller details concerning the armour.

It is a spiritual picture of Christian attentiveness to the procedures of living the godly life. It is necessary for the Christian to trust in the power of God. That was the point of Ephesians 6:10. But there are certain disciplines that have to be followed as well. Paul puts this in picture language. Resisting Satan is a matter of wearing and putting on spiritual armour.

We notice that there are six pieces of armour. Three items of equipment are envisaged as already being worn. *'Stand therefore, having put the truth around your waist as a belt, and having put on the breastplate of righteousness* (6:14), *and having your feet fitted with the readiness of the gospel of peace'* (6:15).

Then there are three pieces of armour that have to be put on in addition to the first three. *'In addition to all this, take up the shield of faith, with which you can extinguish all the burning arrows of the evil one* (6:16). *Take the helmet of salvation and the sword of the Spirit which is the word of God'* (6:17).

Then Paul has something to say about prayer (6:18–20),

but he does not use a piece of armour as an illustration of prayer.

1. **The first piece of armour is 'the belt of truth'**. This brings us to a question of interpretation. Are the pieces of armour something wholly God-given or are they aspects of Christian godliness. For example is 'the truth' to be taken as the truth **of the gospel**, or is it truthfulness of **character**, integrity? The answer is: these items of armour are God's armour. They are firstly pure **gifts** to us; only afterwards do they work themselves out in our own character.

There are several reasons why this must be true. (i) The picture language is taken from Isaiah (see Isaiah 11:5; 59:17) where the items of equipment are pieces of armour worn by the divine warrior. They are aspects of the equipment of the Lord Jesus Christ given to us. (ii) Our truthfulness, righteousness and peace, are surely not capable of standing up to Satan's devices. Christian experience has to be involved in biblical interpretation. Paul's letters are practical; they work out in the way we live. Anyone who thinks he can stand against Satan in the strength of his own morality has not done much standing against Satan!

The 'belt of truth' is the entire gospel. It is 'the truth' that sets us free, the whole counsel of God. No one is ready to resist Satan's attacks who is not held together by God's entire gospel-message.

2. **Second is 'the breastplate of righteousness'**. This is supremely the righteousness of Jesus Christ reckoned to be ours. Philippians 3:4b–9 is the best exposition. There is a righteousness over our lives which comes to us by the faithfulness of Jesus Christ. It is first 'reckoned' to us. When we trust in Jesus Christ God does not 'reckon' or 'count' sin to us (see Romans 4:7–8). To him that does **nothing** but believes on God who justifies the ungodly, his faith is **reckoned** for righteousness. It is this 'reckoned' righteousness that covers us. It is our safety when Satan attacks us. It specially covers our chest; it is a breastplate. The ancient man or woman thought of his feelings and emotions as being

inside his chest. When you are emotional or worried your chest feels tight and your breathing is affected. But God has provided something to protects these inner feelings: the breastplate of Christ's righteousness. Of course we then go on to work out the righteousness in the way we live, but it is first and foremost a gift from God.

3. **Next is to be fitted with 'the shoes of peace'.** When I have the gospel 'strapped on to me', I am at peace with God and am ready to speak the gospel of peace to anyone anywhere.

It must be noticed that these first three items of armour are fixed on at all times. They do not have to be 'taken up' in time of spiritual attack. They should be fixed on to our lives long **before** any special attack of Satan and his forces.

4. **The shield of faith.** To hold up the shield of faith means to apply your faith to any particular problem that comes along. It means to hold up what you know from God's word and stand behind it for protection. The large shield of the Romans was as big as a door. You protect yourself by standing behind the character of God, the promises of God, the power of God. These things that you know are true – you use them as a protective shield.

5. **The helmet of salvation** is our expectation of salvation, our sure and certain knowledge that in this battle victory is certain. The Roman officers who wore brightly coloured feathers on their helmets were famous for their victories. The helmet made them proud to be in the armies of Rome. The Christian 'holds his head high' as one of Christ's soldiers. He knows his Commanding Officer is with him. Victory is sure.

6. **The sword of the Spirit** consists of particular parts of God's word. 'The truth' of 6:14 is the entire gospel; the 'word of God' in 6:17 is special parts of God's word quoted and used as a sword. Jesus used God's word in this way (see Matthew 4:4, 7, 10).

In the midst of battle the Christian has some blessings fixed on to him. And then there are certain things he does in order to stand against the devil. The last three items require watchfulness, wakefulness. The first three are permanent fixtures; the second three are activities which we have to 'take up' and 'put on'.

Chapter 33

Last Words

(Ephesians 6:18–24)

Next Paul has something to say about prayer, but he does not use a piece of armour as an illustration of prayer. It would have been easy for him to say, 'And have with you the spear of prayer'; the Roman soldier always carried a spear and it would have made a nice illustration! But Paul does not do that because prayer is not just a piece of armour alongside other pieces of armour. Everything is to be done with prayer!

'And pray in the Spirit with all prayer and supplication at all times. To this end keep alert with all perseverance and petition for all the saints (6:18), *and for me, that when I open my mouth utterance may be given to me, to make known boldly the mystery of the gospel* (6:19), *for which I am an ambassador in chains. Pray that I may speak boldly, as I ought to speak'* (6:20).

Six points about prayer arise here. (i) Prayer is to be 'in the Spirit'. The Holy Spirit prompts prayer and leads us in prayer. We may use a prayer-list or have some guidelines – as we should – but the Holy Spirit is to be the one who is in control as we pray. We follow the way He leads us. When we begin to pray the first thing we do is remind ourselves that we are in the presence of God, and ask for the help of God's Holy Spirit. (ii) Paul says we must pray 'at all times'. Prayer is supremely vital. It will be of no value for us to try to be strong in the Lord and put on His armour if we do not pray. Without prayer we soon faint and fall. (iii) There are different types of prayer. 'Prayer' is a general term for worship and talking to God. 'Supplication' means casting ourselves on God's mercy. 'Petition' is making requests for ourselves and for others. Paul asks us to pray with 'all prayer' – with every kind of prayer. There is secret prayer; there is church prayer. There is praying with one's mind switched on; there is praying in tongues where the mind is less used. There are 'groanings that cannot be uttered'. (iv) Prayer requires perseverance and watchfulness. This is the supreme secret of the Christian life: to **persevere** in prayer. How easily we give up! We need to programme ourselves. Draw up a time-table. Fix a certain time of the day when you resolve you will get away from other people and pray. It may be before anyone else is awake. It might be long after midnight. (v) We should pray for 'all the saints', Christians known to us far and wide. We are not to use prayer entirely for selfish reasons and purposes. It is a great test of our spirituality – how much do we pray for others? Jesus is our intercessor in heaven. He prays for us all the time. We should be like Jesus. We too should be secret intercessors. (vi) A special theme of prayer is to be the preaching of the gospel. God's preachers need the boldness that comes from the Holy Spirit more than anything else. Paul was in prison but he did not ask that they should pray for his release. There was something far more important than that. He wants boldness to be given to him by the Holy Spirit. The gospel is a 'mystery'. It is something that people do not understand unless the Holy Spirit is at work. Paul is in prison, suffering because of his previous preaching of the gospel. But he just wants more spiritual power to go on preaching. When the Spirit comes down upon us He gives us boldness. It is the supreme mark of the Spirit's being at work in our lives and Paul wants this boldness more than anything else. He pleads with them to pray for this blessing for him.

Paul brings his letter now to an end. He likes to give greetings and communications. *'Now in order that you may know my circumstances, how I am doing, Tychicus the beloved brother and faithful minister in the Lord, will tell you everything'* (6:21). A vital part of Christian fellowship is communication. Rumours and misunderstandings come in unless people are informed. Paul takes the trouble to let his friends know what is happening to him. Also Paul wants them to be encouraged. *'I am sending him to you for this very purpose that you may know how we are, and that he may encourage your hearts'* (6:22). To stay rejoicing is a vital part of the Christian life. Pastors have to keep their people rejoicing. Paul was in prison but he did not let his friends get discouraged about him.

Greetings are important in life. Paul adds: *'Peace be to the brothers and sisters, and love, with faith, from God the Father and the Lord Jesus Christ'* (6:23). Paul feels for his friends as brothers and sisters. He wants them to know the peacefulness and the love of God in their hearts. They on their side will need to exercise faith. *'Grace be with all those who love our Lord Jesus Christ – grace with immortality'* (6:24). The spiritual item we need more than anything is God's grace – His kindly help when we need it and when we think we don't. The last words are best translated 'grace with immortality' (6:24). It is an unusual phrase, but it is Paul's way of speaking of our final reward. When we are raised in glory we shall be clothed with 'immortality', the glory of the resurrection body. It is our final reward; we start living for it even now.

Some Further Reading

Among technical commentaries, those by Marcus Barth (Anchor Bible) and A.T. Lincoln (Word Commentary) may be consulted. F.F. Bruce produced two works on Ephesians (a simple one was once published by Pickering and Inglis; the 'New International Commentary' on Ephesians, Colossians and Philemon is more advanced, and is one of the best on Ephesians).

More devotional and expository are Stott's *The Message of Ephesians* (IVP) and William Hendriksen's *Ephesians*. These are the two that are most suitable for preachers. Charles Hodge's work is still valuable despite its age.

Puritan works include Paul Bayne's seventeenth century commentary. Thomas Goodwin's exposition of Ephesians 1 and some other parts of the letter are tough reading, but magnificent exposition.

In a class of their own are the eight volumes of Dr Martyn Lloyd-Jones (published by Banner of Truth). Every preacher should work through them – but not spend eight years preaching through Ephesians unless he has Lloyd-Jones's gifts!

John Calvin's exposition of Ephesians (not to be confused with his commentary) is excellent.

Works by John Eadie (1861), R.C.H. Lenski, Charles Masson (in French), C.L. Mitton, J.A. Robinson, Rudolf Schnackenburg, B.F. Westcott, are only for those who like to read everything they can get. There are of course dozens of smaller or less significant works.